MICROSOFT WORD FOR SENIORS MADE EASY

Creating Documents Trouble Free

By James Bernstein

Contents

Introduction

Word processing software has been around for almost as long as computers themselves. Microsoft came out with their Windows operating system in 1985 but their word processing software actually came out in 1983. It wasn't until 1989 that Microsoft Word for Windows was released, and it has been the go to word processing software ever since.

Since Windows and Word were both created by Microsoft, it makes sense that they would want to push Windows users to use Word as their word processing software. You might have heard of other word processing software such as Google Docs, LibreOffice, WordPerfect and Apple Pages. Even though these are powerful full featured word processing programs, they are nowhere near as popular as Microsoft Word.

If you have Word installed on your computer, you most likely have other Microsoft programs such as Excel and PowerPoint installed as well since most of the time, people buy Word as part of the Microsoft Office suite of apps even though it is possible to buy Word as a standalone product.

Speaking of Office, you might have heard or read about Office 365. This is Microsoft's subscription-based Office suite that you can use online via your web browser and also as installed programs on your computer. You pay yearly for the subscription but that gets you all the updates for all the Office software as they come out. There is also a free version of Word and other Office apps you can use online called Office for the Web but it's not as powerful as the Office 365 version yet can be just fine for many users.

In this book I will be using the desktop version of Word which most people prefer since it's a bit easier to use and you don't need to worry about storing documents "in the cloud" unless you really want to since it will be an option for you. Once you get the hang of the desktop version of Word, you should also be able to apply your knowledge to the online version and adapt just fine.

Even though Microsoft Word is a very powerful program, I will be sticking with the basics so you can learn how to use the major features of Word and not get overwhelmed by all the advanced tasks you can perform. I will discuss a few of the more advanced features just because I think they are important to at least be aware of. Then once you become proficient with the basics, you can then branch out and learn some of the other features if you choose to do so. So on that note, let's get writing!

Chapter 1 – Word Processor Basics

It is safe to assume that you have an idea of what a word processor is used for since you decided to read this book. You can think of a word processor as a typewriter for your computer. Except when you make a mistake, you don't have to break out the White Out!

Obviously there is more to word processors than typing text but overall, that is the main thing that most people do with them. Sure, you can do things such as create forms, business cards, flyers, posters and more but we are going to focus on getting out text on the page and then I will go over some other things you can do with the software.

Uses for Word Processors at Home & at the Office

The version of Word that you use at home will be the same that you use at the office but how you use it at each location is what will most likely vary. The key thing to take away from this is that you can apply what you learn at the office to your work with Word at home.

Many if not most companies use Word at the office for their employees to do things such as type memos, create fax cover sheets, write reports, create invoices and design media such as flyers and brochures among many other document types. Many other Office applications such as PowerPoint and even Outlook have many of the same features that Word does for doing things such as formatting text and importing images etc.

For home users, you most likely will not be creating the same types of documents as you do at the office. You might use Word at home to write a resume, create holiday cards, make a flyer for a social event, or even create a happy birthday banner that uses several sheets of paper strung together.

Of course you are not limited to creating whatever type of document you like at any location and regardless of where you are using Word, you will most likely never use it to its full potential. I know I never will!

Word vs. WordPad

If you are a Microsoft Windows user, you might have seen or even used the WordPad application that comes included with Windows. This app is free to use and there is no subscription or any pay for service that you need to worry about. If you need to create a basic document and even do things such as add pictures, you can easily do so using WordPad.

Figure 1.1 shows WordPad with a Microsoft Word document open. As you can see at the top of the document, it mentions that WordPad does not support all the features of the document's format. This is common when opening Word files, but you can use WordPad to create its own files that you can also open in Word if needed.

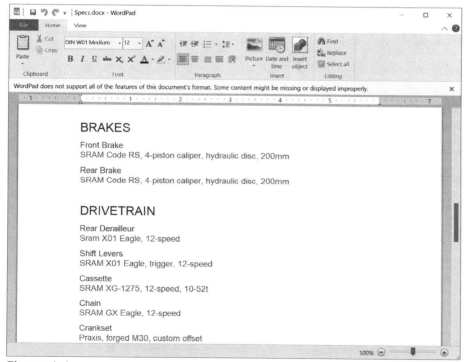

Figure 1.1

If you look at the icons at the top of figure 1.1, you might notice that they are similar to what you see in Word (figure 1.2) but quite a bit limited in comparison. WordPad only has a File, Home and View tab while Word has the same tabs plus several others. I will be discussing the Word Ribbon, which Microsoft named this toolbar and its tabs in chapter 2.

Figure 1.2

Word can also open many more types of files compared to WordPad which is limited to basic Word documents, text files and of course WordPad files.

If you are in a bind and need to create a basic document, then WordPad is a viable option.

Finding and Opening Word

In order to start using Word, of course you will need to be able to open the program first! There are two ways you can open Word to start working. If you double click on a Word document on your computer, it will open the Word program with that particular document loaded.

You can also just open the Word program itself and then start a new document or open an existing program after it has started up. If you are running Windows on your computer, you can click on the Start button and then see if you have an icon for Word in the list and then click on that icon to start Word. If not, then you can look under your All Apps or All Programs section to see if you can find it in the list. Depending on how your computer is configured, it may or may not look similar to figure 1.3.

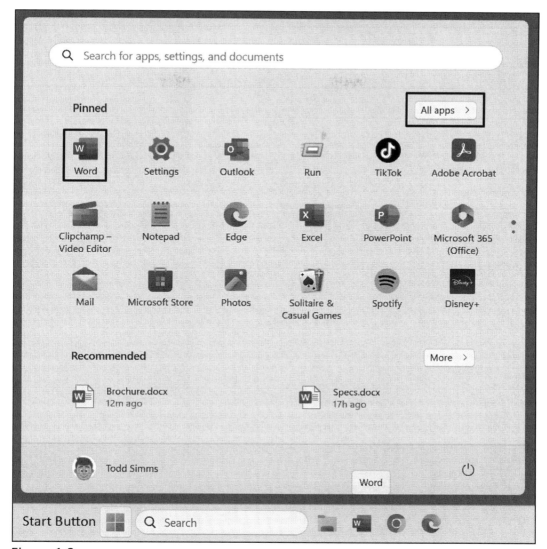

Figure 1.3

You can also click in the search box and do a search for Word and then click on it from the results that appear after you press enter on your keyboard (figure 1.4).

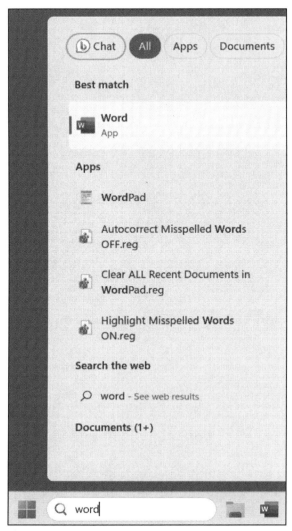

Figure 1.4

You might also get lucky and have an icon on your desktop or on your taskbar as seen in the lower right corner of figure 1.4.

The Word Interface

Before I get too into the ins and outs of how Microsoft Word works, I wanted to take a moment to go over the Word interface so you can see the basic layout. Once you familiarize yourself with the various sections of the Word interface, you will find that using Word becomes much easier.

Figure 1.5 shows a basic Word document and as you can see, there are only a few major areas to focus on when it comes to how the program is laid out.

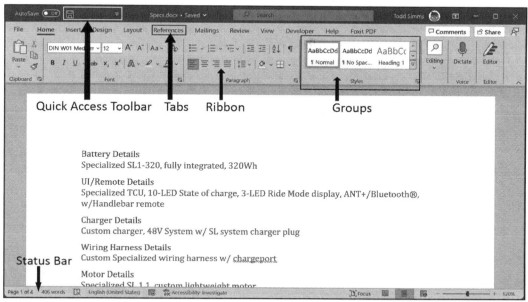

Figure 1.5

At the top left you have the *Quick Access Toolbar* where you can add your more commonly used icons such as save and print.

The section names such as Home, Insert and Design etc. are known as tabs and when you click on a specific tab, the tools and buttons will change accordingly to match that tab. In older versions of Word, these actually looked more like tabs than they do in the current version.

Each section or tab will have its own set of groups within it that are related to that section. For example, the *Home* section has various groups such as *Font*, *Paragraph*, *Styles* and so on. Within these groups you will find tools related to the group itself. For example, the Font group has options to change the font used in the document, as well as its size. You can also make it bold, underlined and italicized etc. Think of fonts as the style of the letters.

Then you have the *Ribbon* which is the whole section of tabs and their groups spanning the entire top area of the Word interface. The Ribbon has been around since Word 2007. If you do not want to see the Ribbon and prefer to have more space to work, then you can click the up arrow (^) at the very right side of the Ribbon to switch to the compact view as seen in figure 1.6.

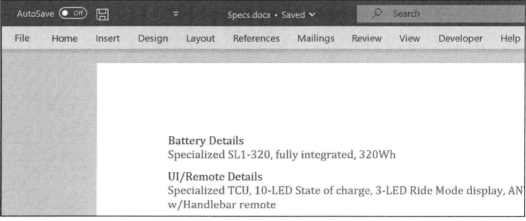

Figure 1.6

Finally, at the bottom left of the Word interface, you have the *status bar* which will show you things such as what page you are on out of how many total pages and the number of words within your document.

Chapter 2 – Word Tabs and Groups

In order to be a proficient Word user, you will need to have an understanding of what the Word tabs and groups are and have a general idea as to what tools are contained in each one. As I mentioned before, you will most likely only be using a small percentage of the features that Word has to offer so don't get overwhelmed when you see how many icons and buttons there are within these sections.

The tabs are the labeled sections at the top of the ribbon and the groups are the named areas within each tab (figure 2.1). In this chapter, I will be going over each of the tabs and the groups within that tab but will be focusing more on what the average Word user will need to know about rather than going over every single item. Also keep in mind that I will be going into more detail about many of the functions of these groups later in the book and this chapter is meant to be an overview of what each tab and group is used for.

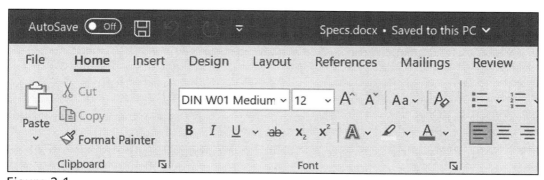

Figure 2.1

File Tab

The File tab is a little different from the other tabs because it does not contain any groups and is not part of the Word Ribbon. When you click on File, you will be taken to a different area of Word where you will be able to do things such as open, save, print and share your document (figure 2.2).

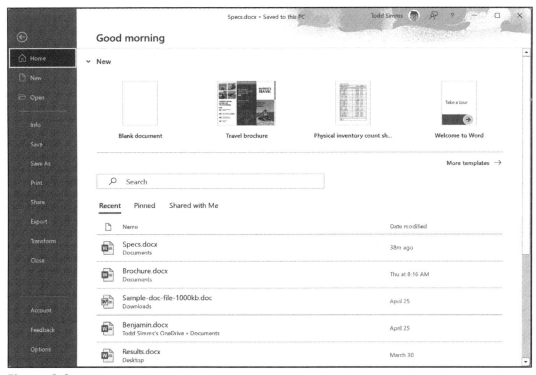

Figure 2.2

On the left side of the File menu, you will have your options to perform tasks such as creating a new document, opening a document, saving your work, printing and so on.

At the top of the File section, you will find templates that can be used as a starting point for creating specific types of documents. I will be discussing templates in chapter 3.

The lower area of the File section will contain a listing of recently opened documents. This gives you an easy way to continue working on a file without having to browse for the document on your hard drive.

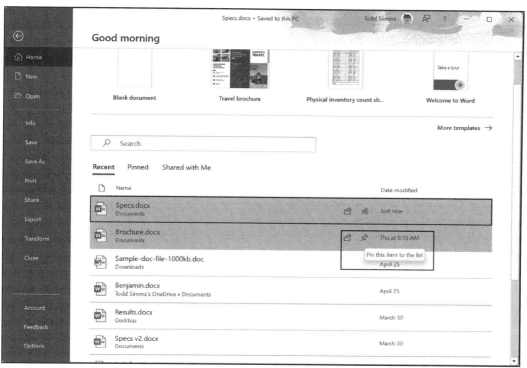

Figure 2.3

You will also have a pinned section that will show you any documents that you have pinned for easy access. Pinning a document keeps it at the top of the list, otherwise it would eventually get replaced with newer, more recent documents. To pin a document, simply hover over its name and then click on the thumbtack icon as seen in figure 2.3.

Clicking on *Open* will also display a listing of your recent documents as well as give you options to open existing documents from your computer or other locations such as the free OneDrive cloud storage account that all Microsoft users get.

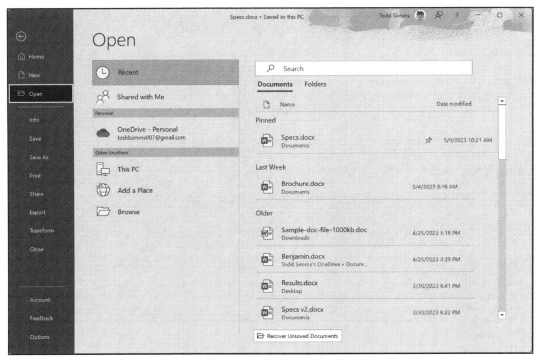

Figure 2.4

If you were to click on *This PC*, you would be shown recent documents once again as well as folders that you have opened documents from in the past.

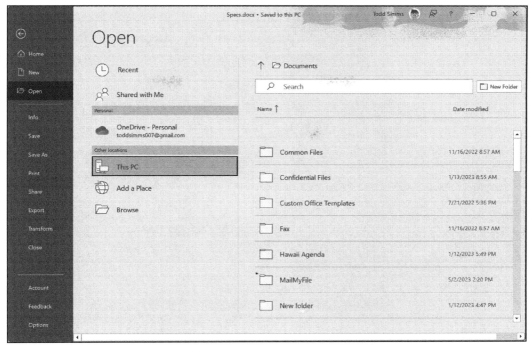

Figure 2.5

If you need to open a document from a folder that is not listed here, you can then click on *Browse* and then navigate to the folder that contains your document.

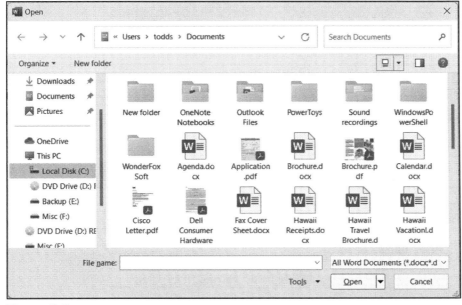

Figure 2.6

The *Info* section might come in handy because it shows you useful information about the currently opened document such as its size, number of pages, number of words, the author, and its created and modified dates.

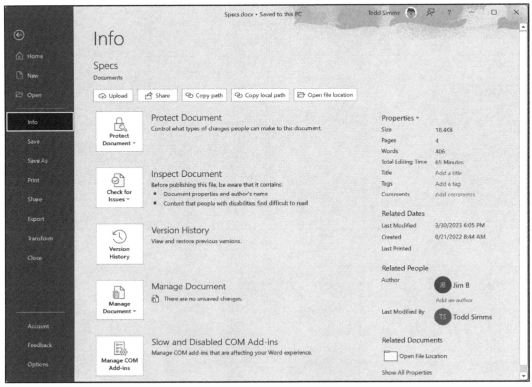

Figure 2.7

At the bottom left corner, you will have the *Options* section where you can configure the Microsoft Word settings (figure 2.8). These settings are beyond the scope of this book but if you want to poke around these options, you might find something that you want to change to make Word work a little better for you. I will briefly cover the Word options in chapter 7.

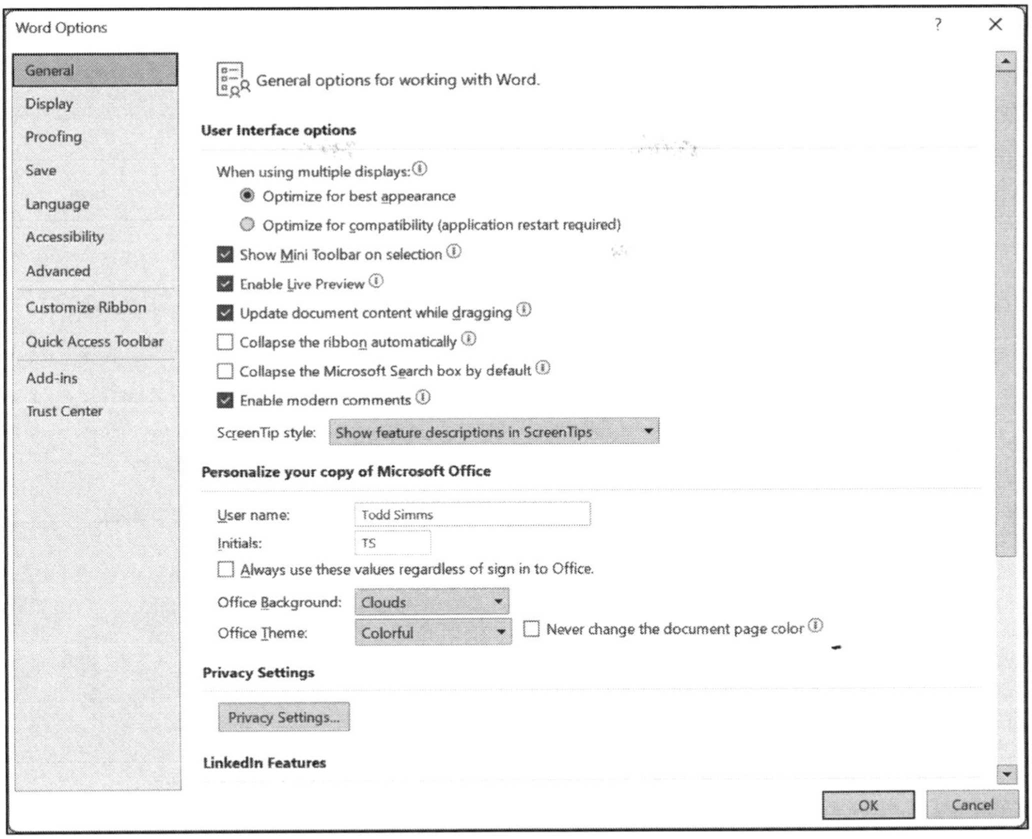

Figure 2.8

Home Tab

The Home tab is where many people spend most of their time, which is probably why they call it the Home tab! Here you will find most of your formatting options as well as tools to do things such as search or check your spelling and grammar. On a side note, if you see a tab or group in any section of this book that you do not have, that doesn't mean you are missing something but rather I have an extra addon installed that placed the additional tab or group within my copy of Word.

Figure 2.9

There are several groups in the Home tab area that you will be accessing on a regular basis and here is an overview of what items you will find in each group.

- **Clipboard** – When you copy text from another document or another program like a web browser and paste it into your document, Word will try and keep the same formatting as the source text that you copied. If you want to change or remove the formatting when you paste it, then you can do so from here. You can also use this section to cut and copy text and images.

- **Font** – Here is where you will go to do things such as choose a different font\typestyle, change its size or color, or make it bold or underlined etc. If you click the arrow icon at the lower right corner of the group, you will be shown additional options for that group. These popout menus are also available for many of the groups within the Word Ribbon.

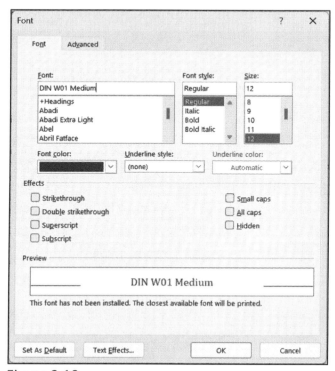

Figure 2.10

- **Paragraph** – By default, Word will left justify your text, meaning it will be aligned to the left side of the page. If you need to change this to centered or right justified, you can do so here. You can also use the Paragraph section to create bulleted or numbered lists which will be discussed in chapter 4.

- **Styles** – Styles are a set of formatting characteristics that you can apply to your text to quickly change its appearance. For example, if you wanted to make your document heading stand out, you could use one of the heading styles by highlighting the text on the page and clicking on that particular style.

- **Editing** – The main tools you will most likely find yourself using here are the find or search option as well as the replace tool. These will be discussed in more detail in chapter 7.

- **Voice** – If you are not the best typist and have a microphone connected to your computer, you can have Word listen to your voice and convert your speech to text on the page.

- **Editor** – Even though Word can check your spelling and grammar as you type, you might find it useful to use the Word Editor to check other aspects of your work such as clarity and conciseness.

Insert Tab

When working in Word, you have the ability to place a variety of objects into your documents such as pictures, shapes, charts, videos, links and much more. The Insert tab is where you will go when you want to insert one of these object types.

Figure 2.11

The Insert tab has many groups, just like you saw with the Home tab but generally these groups do not have an additional pop-out menu like the Home tab does. Here is a brief overview of all the groups within the Insert tab.

- **Pages** – As you probably noticed, Word documents can have several pages and as you type, it will automatically add a new page as you reach the end of the current page. If you want to manually add a new page, you can click on *Blank Page*. If you want to start a new page without filling up the current page, you can click on *Page Break*.

- **Table** – You can add a custom or predefined table to your document as well as insert an Excel spreadsheet type table directly into your document.

- **Illustrations** – It is quite common to insert things such as pictures from your computer or shapes such as boxes or arrows into your document. Once you insert one of these objects into your computer, you can then resize it as needed or in many cases change how the shape itself appears such as turning a square into a rectangle by stretching it out.

- **Add-ins** – Add-ins are extra apps or tools that you can use to add to Word or other Office programs that will give you additional functionality such as more advanced spell checkers or PDF editors for example. You can browse by category or search for a particular type of add-in such as those that can be used for photos as seen in figure 2.12.

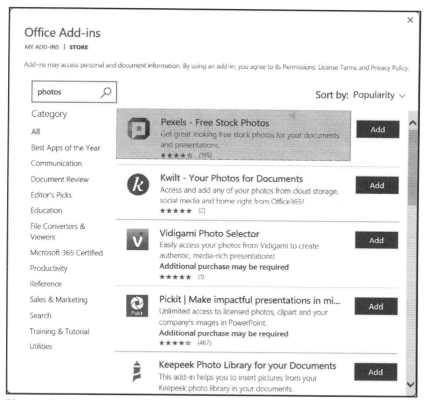

Figure 2.12

- **Media** – Here you can insert an online video by pasting the address for that particular video. For example, if you want to have a YouTube video shown within your document you can paste in the address and then click on the Insert button. Then when someone opens your document, they will be able to play that video right from Word. Of course, this doesn't apply if you print out your document on paper and give it to someone!

Figure 2.13

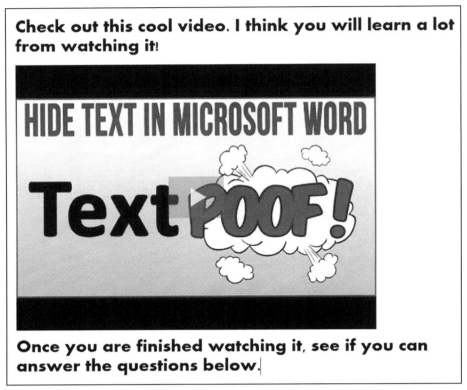

Figure 2.14

- **Links** – It is common to add links to other documents or files to your Word document to make it easy for other people to access them. You can also place links to websites within your document so that when people click on them, they will be taken to that website. More on this in chapter 7.

- **Comments** – If you are sharing documents with other people and have more than one person editing your work, you can add comments to the document that your fellow collaborators can see using this option.

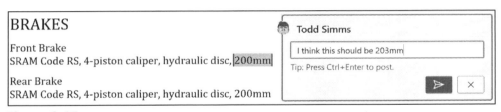

Figure 2.15

- **Header & Footer** – These are used to add things such as chapter titles or reference notes to either the upper (header) or lower (footer) margins of your document. These headers and footers do not reside in the actual body of your document like your other text will. Page numbers will also reside in the footer of a document.

- **Text** – Even though you most likely know how to add text to your document, there are some other ways to do so from the Text group. For example, if you need to add text on top of a picture, you can use a text box. Or if you want to insert the date and time into your document and have it updated automatically, you can use the *Date & Time* feature. The *Object* section is a tool you can use to insert other documents into your Word document so your readers will be able to access those as well.

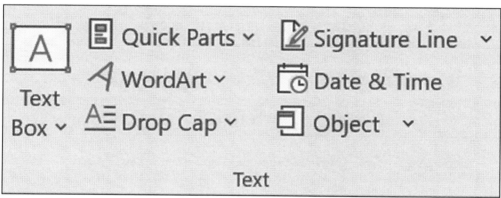

Figure 2.16

- **Symbols** – You most likely won't find yourself using the Equation part of the Symbols group unless you are into complex mathematics! But you might find the need to insert a symbol such as the copywrite or trademark symbol into your document which you can do so from here.

Figure 2.17

Draw Tab

If you ever need to markup your document as if you were writing on it with an actual pen, you can use the tools in the Draw tab. I will be discussing the drawing process in chapter 3, but for now I will go over the tools contained within this tab.

There is a chance you might not have the Draw tab visible on your Ribbon. If so, all you need to do is right click any blank spot on the Ribbon and choose *Customize the Ribbon* and check the box for the Draw tab as seen in figure 2.18.

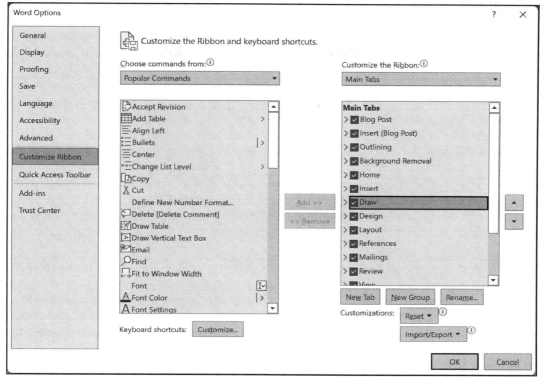

Figure 2.18

As you can see in figure 2.19, the Draw tab does not have as many tools as many of the other tabs, but it can still come in very handy.

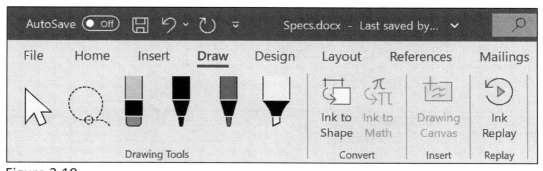

Figure 2.19

Here is what each group from the Draw tab can be used for.

- **Drawing Tools** – This group contains basic tools such as a pen, marker, highlighter and eraser. The arrow tool can be used to drag

- and resize your drawing and the lasso tool is used to select one or more ink shapes after you draw them.

- **Convert** – This can be used to convert drawings to actual refined shapes or hand drawn equations into typed numbers and symbols.

- **Insert** – Here you can insert a canvas into your document which you can think of as a container for your drawings and then you can draw inside that canvas to have all your drawings contained within that box so you can do things such as move everything as one item.

- **Replay** – The Replay feature will show you an animated replay of the last thing you drew on the page.

Design Tab

Microsoft Word comes with a default configuration regarding what fonts, styles, colors etc. are used in all your documents. Of course you can manually change all of these attributes as needed, or you can change the overall design of your document in one place from this area.

The tools in the Design tab are broken down into different sections that allow you to change these default settings and even have them apply to future documents.

Figure 2.20

Here is what you will find in each group.

- **Themes** – Themes are a preconfigured combination of colors, styles and fonts that you can have applied to your document. When you click on the Themes button, you will be shown the various options and a preview of how they will look when applied to your document.

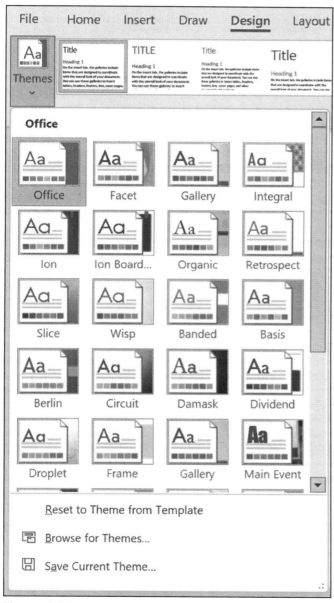

Figure 2.21

Figure 2.22 shows a sample document with the default theme applied and figure 2.23 shows the same document after changing the theme.

Installing the Explorer Patcher for Windows 11 Software

The first step in getting the Quick Launch Toolbar back is to install the ExplorerPatcher software that you can download here. When you are on the Github website, look for a line that says Download the latest version of the setup program under the How-to section. You will then download a file named ep_setup.exe.

Now you will run the executable file that you have downloaded to install the ExplorerPatcher software. You won't be prompted with any questions about installation paths etc. and the software will simply install itself silently.

You will know its complete when you see your start button and other taskbar icons on the left side of the taskbar. You will also see a different looking Start button.

Figure 2.22

Installing the Explorer Patcher for Windows 11 Software

The first step in getting the Quick Launch Toolbar back is to install the ExplorerPatcher software that you can download here. When you are on the Github website, look for a line that says Download the latest version of the setup program under the How-to section. You will then download a file named ep_setup.exe.

Now you will run the executable file that you have downloaded to install the ExplorerPatcher software. You won't be prompted with any questions about installation paths etc. and the software will simply install itself silently.

You will know its complete when you see your start button and other taskbar icons on the left side of the taskbar. You will also see a different looking Start button.

Figure 2.23

- **Document Formatting** – The Document Formatting group is used to apply preconfigured styles to your document. You can click on any one of the selections to have it instantly applied to your work. The Colors, Fonts, Spacing and Effects options are used to change only those specific attributes rather than the entire theme. One thing you can do is apply a theme and then customize it by changing one of these other options.

- **Page Background** – As you have probably noticed, your Word documents will have a white background representing a sheet of paper. If you want your page to be a different color, you can use the Page Color option to change it. If you plan to print your document, I don't recommend changing the color because it will use a lot of ink since it will have to cover the entire sheet of paper with whatever color you choose. By default, Word shouldn't print backgrounds unless you enable that option.

  Watermarks are used to add faint text to the background such as the word draft or confidential as shown in figure 2.24.

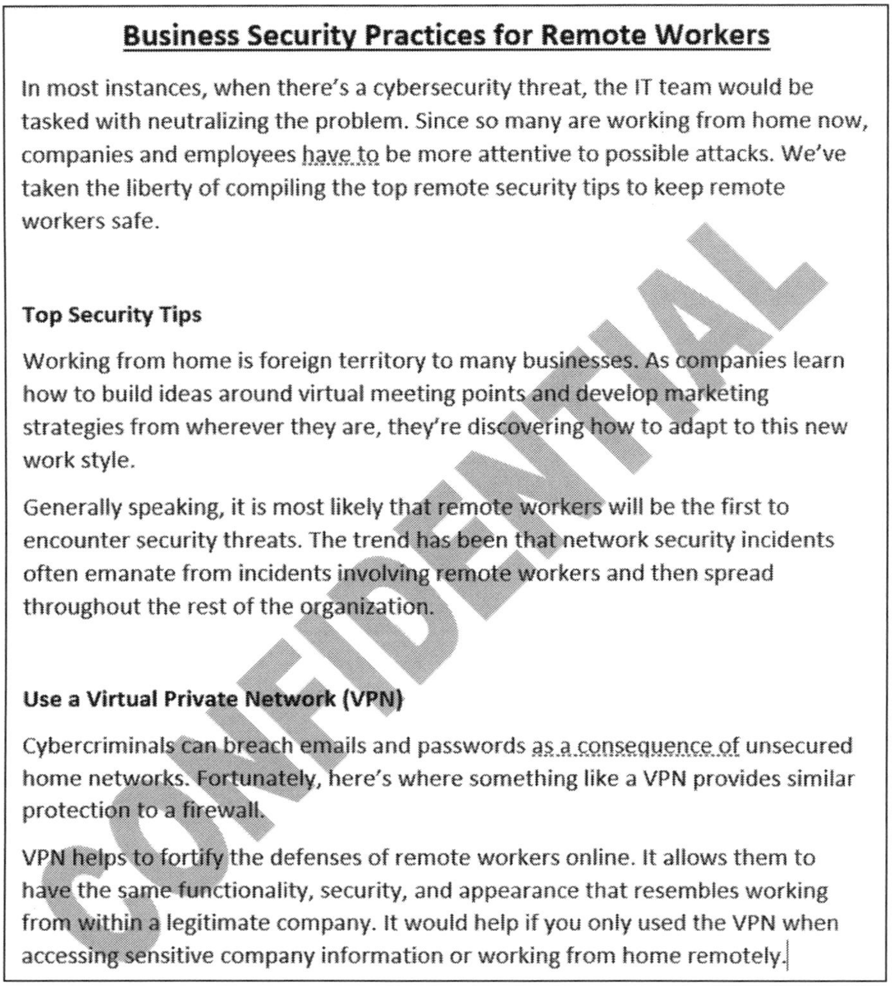

Business Security Practices for Remote Workers

In most instances, when there's a cybersecurity threat, the IT team would be tasked with neutralizing the problem. Since so many are working from home now, companies and employees have to be more attentive to possible attacks. We've taken the liberty of compiling the top remote security tips to keep remote workers safe.

Top Security Tips

Working from home is foreign territory to many businesses. As companies learn how to build ideas around virtual meeting points and develop marketing strategies from wherever they are, they're discovering how to adapt to this new work style.

Generally speaking, it is most likely that remote workers will be the first to encounter security threats. The trend has been that network security incidents often emanate from incidents involving remote workers and then spread throughout the rest of the organization.

Use a Virtual Private Network (VPN)

Cybercriminals can breach emails and passwords as a consequence of unsecured home networks. Fortunately, here's where something like a VPN provides similar protection to a firewall.

VPN helps to fortify the defenses of remote workers online. It allows them to have the same functionality, security, and appearance that resembles working from within a legitimate company. It would help if you only used the VPN when accessing sensitive company information or working from home remotely.

Figure 2.24

Page borders are a nice way to add a little style to your document by adding a preconfigured or custom border around your text. I will be discussing page borders in chapter 4.

Layout Tab

Page layout is an important thing to consider when creating a Word document. You should be thinking about what you plan to do with your document, so you know how to set it up properly. For example, one thing to consider would be if you or someone else will be printing it and if so, will the page size you have configured be correct for the printer type and paper size that your document will require.

There are many other settings you can configure from the Layout tab to make sure that your document looks its best and is easy to read. And if you plan to add objects like pictures and shapes, you will most likely find yourself here since it has some useful tools to help keep them in the right place within your document.

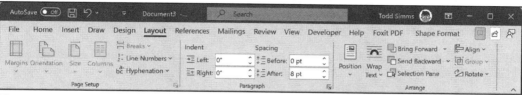

Figure 2.25

Here are the groups you will find within the Layout tab.

- **Page Setup** – Here you will find many useful settings to help ensure that your page settings are correct for printing or exporting etc. You can set things such as the margins, orientation (portrait or landscape) and paper size. I will be discussing page setup in more detail in chapter 4.

- **Paragraph** – If you need to indent a paragraph or change the spacing between them, you can do so from here.

- **Arrange** – You might have a situation where you have a picture in your document and then want to place a shape or text box over it and realize that the picture is covering that shape or text.

  Figure 2.26 shows a star shape covering the text that has been placed on top of the photo. To fix this, I will need to reorder the star shape and the text. To do this, I can either click on the star and send it backward or click on the text and send it forward. The results are shown in figure 2.27.

Figure 2.26

Figure 2.27

You can also use the *Position* tool to tell Word how you want your picture or other object to be aligned with any text that might be around it, otherwise your text will either be above the picture, below it, or both. You can also use the *Wrap Text* tool as another way to align text with objects.

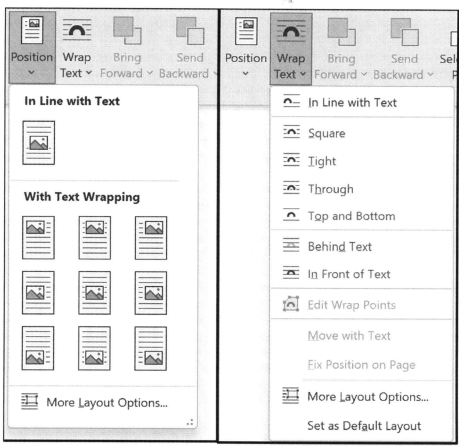

Figure 2.28

Another option here worth mentioning is the *Rotate* tool which you can use on objects in your document to change their orientation.

References Tab

For the average user, the References tab is not someplace you will be visiting too often. It is mainly used for people who are writing books or papers where they have obtained information from other sources and need to cite that in their work.

Figure 2.29

Here is an overview of the groups in the References tab just in case you think you might need to use some of the features.

- **Table of Contents** – Word can automatically create a table of contents from your document as long as you assign outline levels to the text that you want to be used in the TOC.

- **Footnotes** – Footnotes are used to add additional information about a section of your document at the bottom of the page.

- **Research** – Word can use this to go online to find additional information about some text or an image etc. within your document.

- **Citations and Bibliography** – If you have used other people's work in your document and want to give them credit for it, you can add a citation here. This is also where you can insert a bibliography about these works that you have referenced in your document.

- **Captions** – Captions can be applied to pictures etc. and then you can reference those captions at other locations in your document.

- **Index** – Here is where you can create an index for your document as well as tell Word what items you want to be added to that index.

- **Table of Authorities** – This is used to list all the sources cited in a legal document and also to note the page numbers on which each source has been cited.

Mailings Tab

The Mailings tab is another area you might not ever find yourself using unless you plan on printing envelopes or labels. It is also where you go to perform a mail merge which is the process of taking data such as names and addresses from a spreadsheet and using it to print out multiple envelopes, labels, or letters.

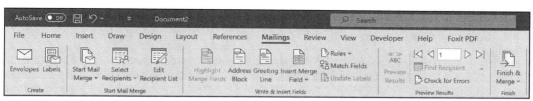

Figure 2.30

Here are the tools you will find within the Mailings tab.

- **Create** – If you want to print out one or more envelopes or labels, you can do so from here. Word will take the text from your document and automatically add it to your envelope or label, or you can use a blank document and add your own.

  Figure 2.31 shows the envelope settings, and you can click on the *Options* button to choose a different size envelope. Figure 2.32 shows the envelope in Word which is now ready to print.

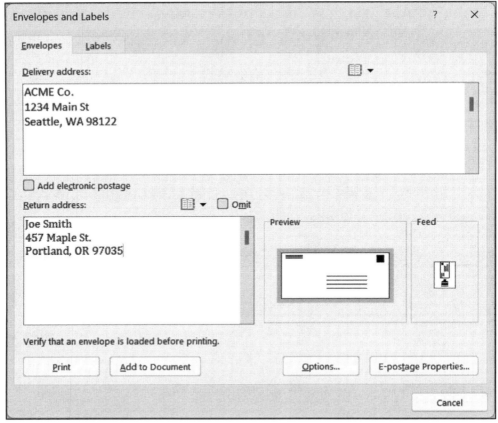

Figure 2.31

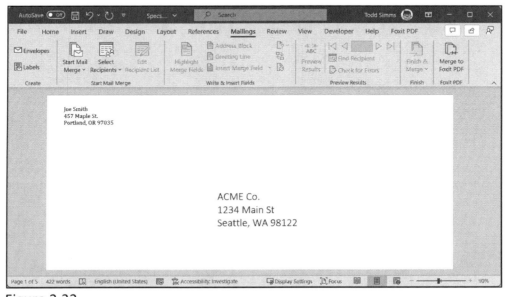

Figure 2.32

You can also perform the same steps for labels and choose from hundreds of label templates from various label manufacturers.

- **Start Mail Merge** – Mail merge is the process of taking a list of names and addresses from another document such as a spreadsheet and applying them to envelopes and labels all at once so they can then be printed.

- **Write & Insert Fields** – This is used to create custom text fields in the document that is set to receive mail merge information.

- **Preview Results** – This is used to preview your merged documents in case you need to make any changes before completing the mail merge.

- **Finish** – Once everything looks good, you can click the *Finish & Merge* button to start the mail merge process.

Review Tab

The Review tab is where you can go to do things such as check your spelling and grammar, translate your document, or comment and track changes on shared documents.

Figure 2.33

The most commonly used tools here are most likely the spelling and grammar checker but I will now give you an overview of all the groups within the Review tab.

- **Proofing** – The Proofing group contains the *Editor* which not only checks spelling and grammar but will also check your document for

41

things such as clarity, conciseness and formality. I will be discussing the Editor in detail in chapter 5.

- **Speech** – If you would like to have your document read aloud to you, you can use this feature to do so. You might find this helpful when it comes to proofreading your work.

- **Accessibility** – This is used to check your work against a set of rules that are used to determine if your document might contain issues that would make it hard for people with certain disabilities to read.

- **Language** – If you need to change the language used for proofing your document from the default, you can do so here. You can also use the *Translator* feature to translate a section of your document or the entire document to a different language.

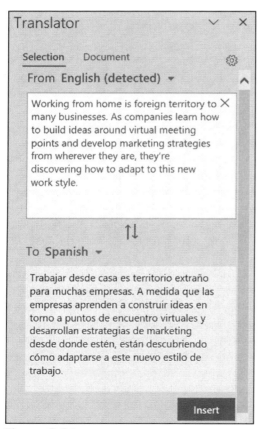

Figure 2.34

- **Comments** – Comments are used to make notes about a particular section of your document. Once you make a comment and send the document to someone else or share it, they will be able to read your comments as well as add their own. This is the same feature that you can also access from the *Insert* tab.

- **Tracking** – If you are sharing a document and collaborating with others, you might want to see what changes they have been making to your document. If you enable tracking, this will show you who has made what changes to your document.

- **Changes** – Here you can accept or reject changes made by others on shared documents.

- **Compare** – Compare can be used to compare two versions of a document to see how they differ. You can also merge two versions of the same document into one new document. When using this feature, you can select the documents to compare and view them side by side with the differences highlighted.

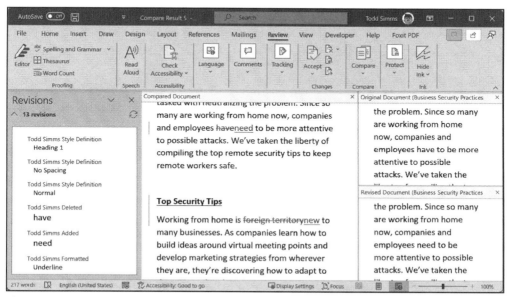

Figure 2.35

- **Protect** – If your document contains information that you do not want to be changed by other people, you can use the tools here to restrict or block editing.

- **Ink** – If you recall the section on the Draw tab, you might remember how you can use the markers and highlighters to actually draw on your document as if you were using an actual pen. If you want to hide your "ink" markups, you can do so from here.

View Tab

The View tab is one of the areas in Word that you will probably find yourself using more than some of the other tabs. The tools contained here are primarily used to change how your document is displayed on the screen so you can make it easier to work with.

Figure 2.36

Here is a breakdown of the groups in the View tab.

- **Views** – By default, Word uses the *Print Layout* view because it represents how your document will look when it is printed. But if you want to work on your document using a different view such as *Outline* or *Draft*, you can do so by clicking on the appropriate button.

- **Immersive** – The tools here are meant to be used to help you focus on your work, especially when proofreading. The *Focus* option will remove the Ribbon so all you see is your document. You can press the *Esc* key on your keyboard to get back to the normal view.

The *Immersive Reader* tool is used to change the way your document looks to make it easier to read. Figure 2.37 shows how this tool changes the line and character spacing and can also break down words to show syllables. You can also have it highlight one line at a time or change the page background color. You will also notice that you can use the Read Aloud feature from here as well.

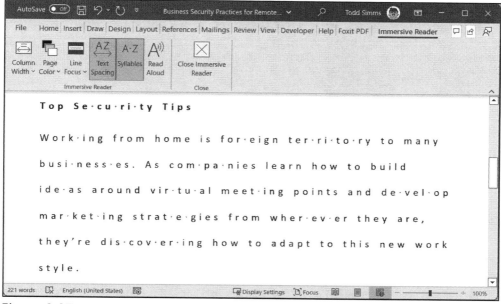

Figure 2.37

- **Page Movement** – By default, when navigating through the pages in your document, Word will scroll the pages vertically (up and down), but if you want to scroll horizontally (side to side), you can change this setting here.

- **Show** – Word has the option to show an on-screen ruler and gridlines to help you with sizing and placement for things like images and shapes. The *Navigation Pane* is used to show headings, page thumbnails and search results.

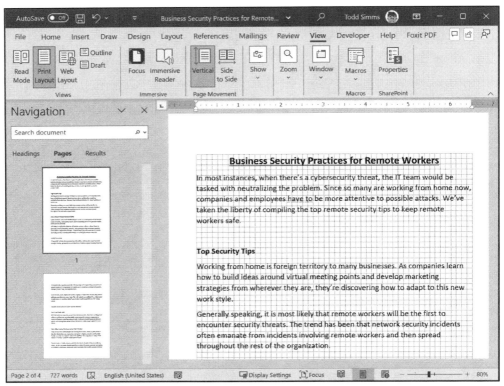

Figure 2.38

- **Zoom** – Depending on how much of the page you want to see on the screen, or how good your eyesight is, you might want to change the zoom level of your document on the screen. You can do so from here or use the zoom slider at the lower right corner of the page.

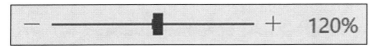

Figure 2.39

- **Window** – The window feature comes in handy if you want to work on two different parts of your document at the same time but don't want to have to scroll up and down the document each time you want to get to each section.

Figure 2.40 shows the same document open but split so I can then scroll to different parts of it independently and then make changes.

Changes made to either the top or bottom window are made within the same document.

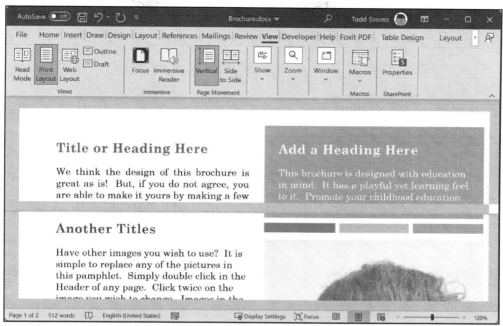

Figure 2.40

You can also use the *View Side by Side* option to have two different documents open next to each other to make it easy to compare the two.

The *Switch Windows* button can be used to quickly switch between open documents.

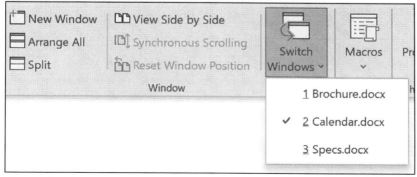

Figure 2.41

- **Macros** – Macros are a series of commands used to automate frequently used tasks.

- **SharePoint** – This option will take you to the Info section like you saw under the File tab so you can view the properties of your document.

Picture Format Tab

One thing you might notice about the Picture Format tab is that you don't have one on your Ribbon! If that is the case, don't worry because it only shows up if you have a picture inserted into your document and you have it selected\highlighted.

Figure 2.42

All the groups in the Picture Format tab are geared towards formatting your picture and the text around it. Here is what you can do with the tools in each group.

- **Adjust** – If you need to do things such as remove the background from a picture or adjust its brightness or color, you can do so from there.

- **Picture Styles** – Here you can add various style attributes to your pictures such as borders, effects and custom layouts as seen in figure 2.43.

Figure 2.43

- **Accessibility** – If you want to make your picture more accessible for someone with impaired vision, you can add some alternative text to describe your picture that can be read by screen reading software.

- **Arrange** – These are the same options you saw earlier in the chapter where you can change the placement of your picture and other objects to make one be on top of the other etc.

- **Size** – Here you can type in a custom size (width and height) as well as crop your image. To crop a picture, simply drag the sides or corners with your mouse to the area you wish to keep visible and then release the mouse (figure 2.44).

Figure 2.44

Quick Access Toolbar

At the upper left corner of the screen, you will see some icons for tasks such as save and undo\redo. This section is called the Quick Access Toolbar and is meant to be used as a place to store your more commonly used tools. You can think of it as being similar to your favorites or bookmarks in your web browser.

If you click on the down arrow on the right side of the other icons, you will be shown a listing of additional commands that you can add to your Quick Access Toolbar if you think they are something you would commonly use.

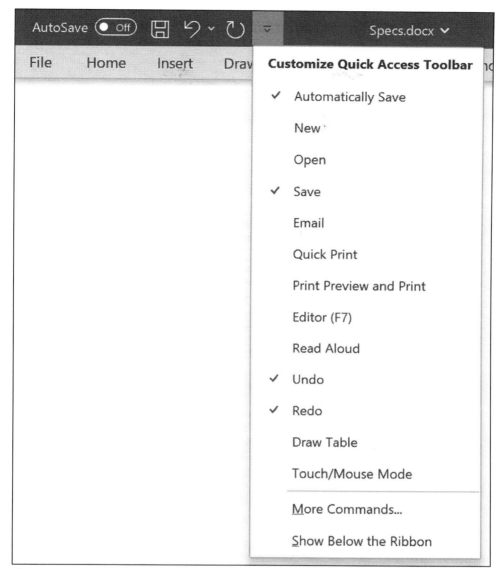

Figure 2.45

If you click on *More Commands*, you will be taken to the Quick Access Toolbar settings (figure 2.46). Here you can add additional commands that might not be on the drop down menu shown in figure 2.45.

I will click on *Find* and then the *Add* button to have it added to the column on the right and then do the same for *Open* and click the *OK* button.

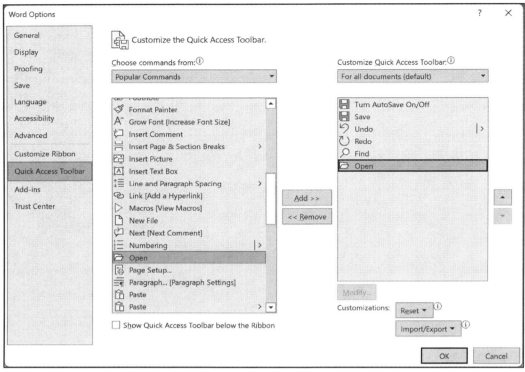

Figure 2.46

Now you can see that I have the Find and Open commands shown in my Quick Access Toolbar for easy access.

Figure 2.47

You can right click on any of the icons in the toolbar and choose *Remove from Quick Access Toolbar* to have them removed from your toolbar.

Chapter 3 – Creating a Document

Now that you have an idea of where to find the tools you need to work on your documents, it is time to create a new document and start adding content.

When you open Word, you will be prompted to either create a new blank document, start a new document using a template or open a file on which you have previously worked.

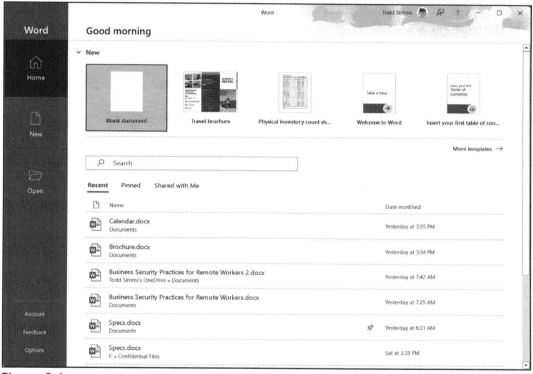

Figure 3.1

Another way to open Word is to double click on a Word file from your computer itself. When you do this, it will open Word with that document opened to the last place you saved it.

Templates

I will be starting with a new blank document for this chapter, but I wanted to first discuss templates in case you wanted to try some of them out.

You can think of templates as documents with preconfigured text, colors and images that you can then customize to suit your needs. Once you open a template you can change any text, pictures or formatting and add or remove anything you need or do not need.

To open a template, go to the *File* menu and choose *New* and you will be shown some sample templates, and to the right of these samples, you can click on the *More templates* link to be taken to the main templates page.

From here you can choose one of the suggested templates, browse templates in the suggested search categories or do your own custom search for a specific template.

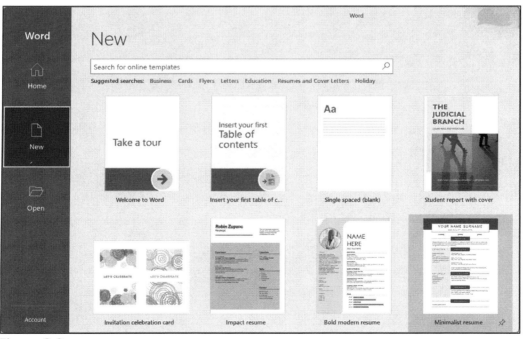

Figure 3.2

For example, if I type **resume** in the search box, I will be shown the available resume templates that I can then download and use on my computer.

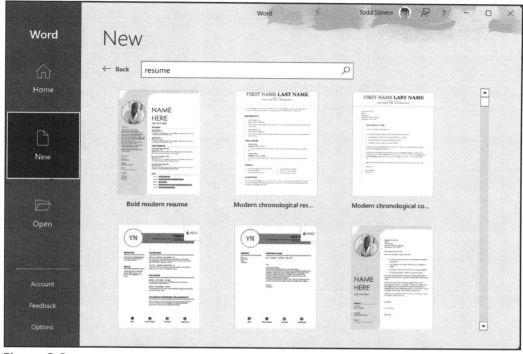

Figure 3.3

I will then choose the first resume template and then Word will open the file on my computer. I can then edit the document as I see fit and save it on my computer so I will have my own copy.

Figure 3.4

Page Size, Margins and Orientation

Before starting your new document, you might want to take a moment to think about what you will be doing regarding printing it or sharing it with others. Then once you figure this out, you can set up your page size and margins.

The page size is important for printing since it will need to match the size of the physical paper you are going to print your document on to make sure everything fits. If you never plan to print your document or share it with others, then it's not as critical.

The default page size for new Word documents is 8.5 x 11 inches, also known as letter size. If you go to the *Layout* tab and then to the *Page*

Setup group, then you will see an icon that says *Size* and if you click on it, you can select a different page size. If you do not want to use one of the built in page sizes, you can then click on *More Paper Sizes* and type in the exact size you need in inches.

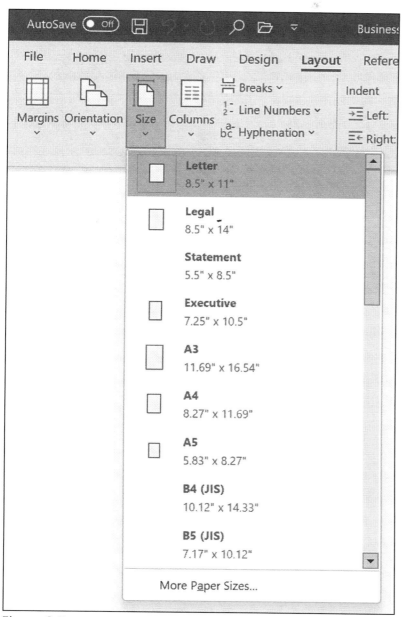

Figure 3.5

If you have already started adding content to your document and then change the page size, you might have to do some adjustments with text and images to make sure they look correct with your new page size.

Margins are another important thing to consider if you or someone else will be printing your document. Margins are the blank space between your text and the edge of the page.

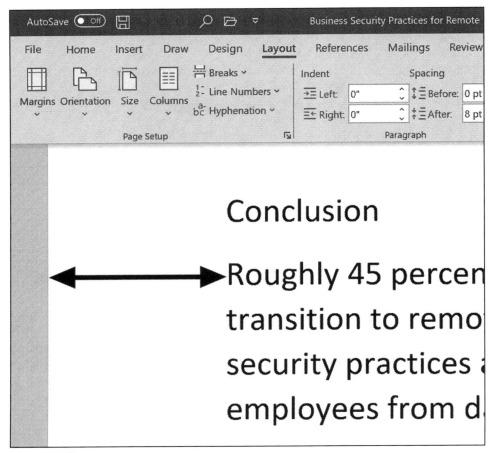

Figure 3.6

If your margins are too narrow, then your document might look odd because the text will be too close to the edge of the page. Then depending on your printer, some of the text might get cut off during the printing process because your printer might not be able to print that close to the edge of the paper.

The default margin size for new Word documents is one inch on all sides of the paper but if you want to increase or decrease this setting, you can go to the *Layout* tab and *Page Setup* group once again. Then you will be able to choose a different page layout from one of the built in settings or you can click on *Custom Margins* to type in your own specific margins.

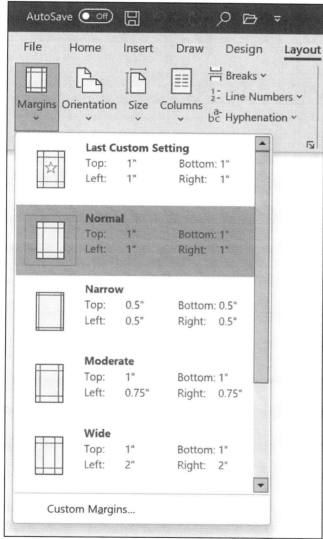

Figure 3.7

When you create a new blank Word document, it will be set to portrait mode which means the page is taller than it is wider. If you want to configure your page to be facing the other direction, you can change it to landscape mode. Figure 3.8 shows you where this can be done, and you can see a preview of how the page will look when you click on the *Orientation* button.

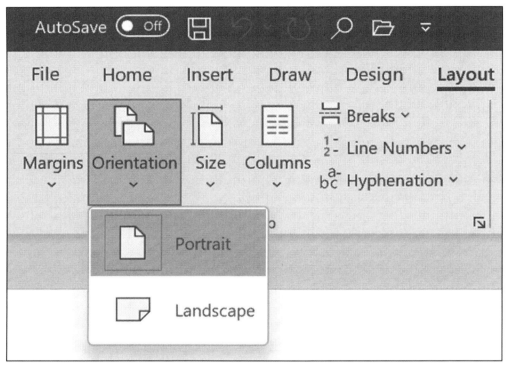

Figure 3.8

Adding Text to Your Document

The main reason for using Microsoft Word is to create documents with text, images and other objects. When you first create a new document, you will most likely be adding text before anything else.

When you click your mouse within your blank document, you should see a flashing cursor indicating the starting point for where your text will be added as you type. The cursor should follow your typing and end up at the end of your line of text as seen in figure 3.9.

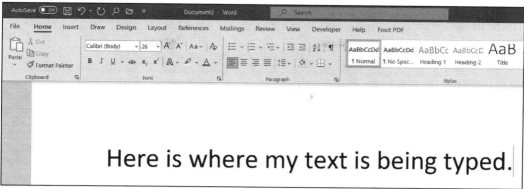

Figure 3.9

You might find that you accidentally click somewhere else on the page and when you start typing, your text is not being placed where you intended it to be. With that in mind, try to be aware of where your cursor is currently placed so you always know where your new text will be added. And if you need to add text to a different location or even in the middle of a sentence, you can simply click the location on the page with your mouse to put the flashing cursor there so you can add your text as needed.

Highlighting Text
One important and very useful thing you should know how to do is highlight text because this makes it much easier to change and delete your text as you make changes.

To highlight text, simply place the mouse cursor at the beginning or end of the text you wish to highlight and click and hold while dragging to the left or right. Once the text is highlighted, simply release the mouse button.

Figure 3.10 shows that I have highlighted the text that says **all people** within a paragraph. Now that it is highlighted, I can delete it by pressing the Delete key on my keyboard and then either leave it as is or add some replacement text. An even faster way is to start typing while the original text is highlighted, and you will notice that it will instantly be replaced by what you are now typing without needing to delete the text first.

Get a Suitable Antivirus Program

It's best to ensure that all people working from home know that antivirus software on personal devices is a must. It decreases the chance that a virus can destroy phones, computers, laptops, and other special programs installed on this equipment.

Figure 3.10

Figure 3.11 shows my replacement text (any employees) that has taken the place of the original text that I had highlighted. You will also notice that the cursor is now at the end of the word employees since that is the last thing I had typed.

Get a Suitable Antivirus Program

It's best to ensure that any employees working from home know that antivirus software on personal devices is a must. It decreases the chance that a virus can destroy phones, computers, laptops, and other special programs installed on this equipment.

Figure 3.11

Another way to remove text is to place the cursor to the right of the text you wish to remove and then press the *Backspace* key on your keyboard until the text has been deleted.

One thing you really need to know when it comes to using Word and many other programs is that you have the ability to undo changes you have made as well as redo changes you have reversed or undone. Let's say you deleted a paragraph of text or changed some wording and then realized that this is not what you intended to do. So rather than retype what you had there before, you can simply undo the changes you just made.

At the top left of the Word interface in the Quick Access Toolbar, you will find the undo and redo icons. Each time you click on Undo, it will revert the last change you made and then the change before that and so on. Then if you change your mind again and want to "undo your undo", you can click the redo button to go forward.

Figure 3.12

I like to use shortcut keys for this purpose rather than clicking the undo and redo buttons because to me it's faster. For Windows, you can press **Ctrl-Z** for undo and **Ctrl-Y** for redo. For Mac users, it is **Command-Z** for undo and for redo it is **Command-Shift-Z**.

Styles
Styles are types of formatting characteristics that you can apply to text with a click of the mouse. If you go to the *Home* tab, you will see samples of the styles that come included with Word. By default, Word will use the Normal style for new documents unless you change it to one of the other types.

When you look at the Styles section, you will be able to see a preview of what that style would look like if you were to use it.

Figure 3.13

To apply a style to existing text you will first need to highlight the text that you want it to apply to. Figure 3.14 shows my document with the default Normal style applied to the text.

Business Security Practices for Remote Workers

In most instances, when there's a cybersecurity threat, the IT team would be tasked with neutralizing the problem. Since so many are working from home now, companies and employees have to be more attentive to possible attacks. We've taken the liberty of compiling the top remote security tips to keep remote workers safe.

Top Security Tips

Working from home is foreign territory to many businesses. As companies learn how to build ideas around virtual meeting points and develop marketing strategies from wherever they are, they're discovering how to adapt to this new work style.

Figure 3.14

Now if I highlight this text and then choose the *Strong* style, you can see how it changes the text by making it bold as well as changing the font.

Business Security Practices for Remote Workers

In most instances, when there's a cybersecurity threat, the IT team would be tasked with neutralizing the problem. Since so many are working from home now, companies and employees have to be more attentive to possible attacks. We've taken the liberty of compiling the top remote security tips to keep remote workers safe.

Top Security Tips

Working from home is foreign territory to many businesses. As companies learn how to build ideas around virtual meeting points and develop marketing strategies from wherever they are, they're discovering how to adapt to this new work style.

Figure 3.15

I prefer to change the text formatting within my documents manually since I am not a big fan of any of the built in Word styles. I will be discussing formatting in chapter 4.

Inserting Pictures

It is very common to add pictures to your documents, especially if you are creating something like a brochure or newsletter. There are several places you can get your pictures from depending on your needs.

If you go to the *Insert* tab and then click on *Pictures*, you will see that you can add a picture from your computer (this device), stock images and from an online source.

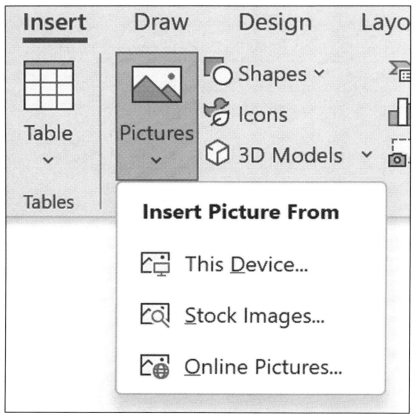

Figure 3.16

I will skip the first option for now since that will be how I will be adding my pictures in a moment. The stock images option lets you choose from pictures that have been created for others to use free of charge. There are several categories to choose from such as images, stickers and illustrations.

All you need to do is type in what kind of picture you are looking for in the search box and you will then be shown results that match your search (figure 3.17). You can then click on the different categories to find content that matches your search term.

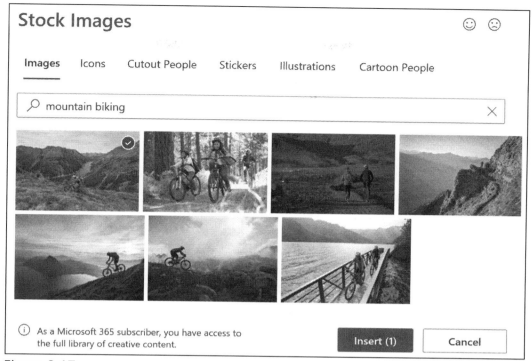

Figure 3.17

Once you find the picture or pictures you want to add to your document, simply click on the *Insert* button to have them added. I recommend placing your cursor in the location where you want the picture to be placed before doing this step.

The *Online Pictures* option goes out to the internet to find pictures that match your search term. You will not have the different categories like you do for stock images though.

If you check the box for *Creative Commons only*, you will be shown results that are free (legal) to use within your document. If you are working on a personal document or something that will not be used as an advertisement or publication that will be sold, you should be fine using any pictures you find and don't really need to check the Creative Commons only box.

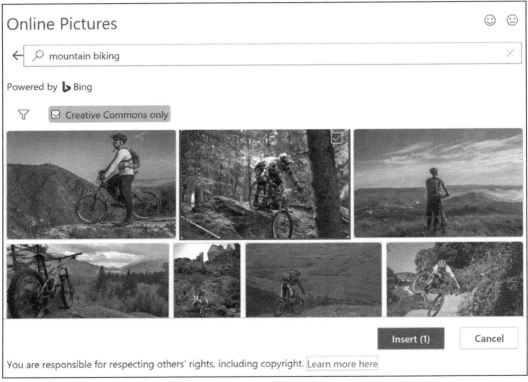

Figure 3.18

Since I will be using a picture from my computer, I will use the *this device* option and browse to the folder on my hard drive where I have the picture I want to add to my document. Once I find it, I can either double click it or select it and click the *Insert* button (figure 3.19).

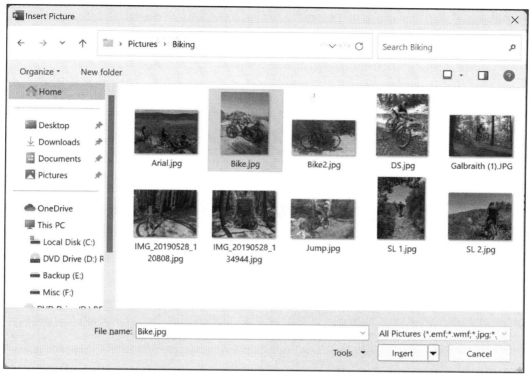

Figure 3.19

Now my picture has been placed in my document (figure 3.20), but one thing to keep in mind is that Word treats it sort of like text when it comes to how it's inserted into my document. For example, if I were to place my cursor above it and press the Enter key on my keyboard, the picture would move down the page just like text will do.

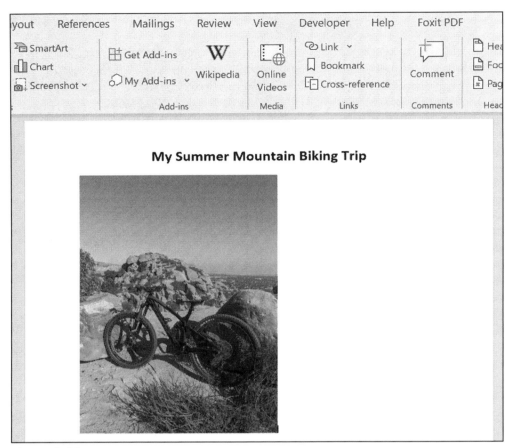

Figure 3.20

What I want to do next is crop my picture and then center it below my title text on the page. First, I will double click the picture to bring up the *Picture Format* tab and then select the *Crop* option in the *Size* group.

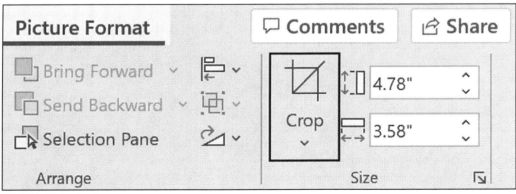

Figure 3.21

Now I will have black bars on the sides and corners of my picture which I can click on with my mouse and hold as I drag to crop out the section of my picture that I do not want to be showing any longer.

Figure 3.22

Figure 3.23 shows the results of my crop and if I change my mind, I can go through the same process and bring back the section of the picture I had previously cropped out since Word will actually leave the entire picture within your document and just keep the cropped section hidden.

My Summer Mountain Biking Trip

Figure 3.23

Now I need to center my picture under my title text and to do this I will select the picture, go to the *Home* tab and click on the *Center* button in the *Paragraph* group as seen in figure 3.24.

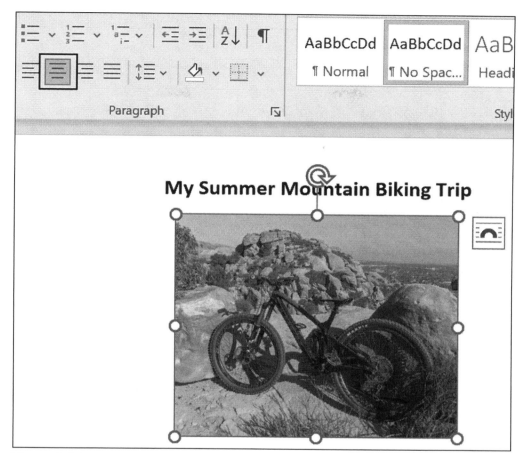

Figure 3.24

You might have noticed the icon that appears next to your picture when you select it and are wondering what it is used for. This is the *Layout Options* icon and when you click on it, you can do things such as have your image be on top of or behind text so you can move it freely with your mouse rather than having it stay aligned with your text. You can also set up text wrapping which will make your text surround your picture for a more custom look.

Figure 3.25

Inserting Shapes

When working with pictures and other inserted items within your document, you might find the need to add a particular shape such as an arrow or box on top of the picture to highlight part of it for example.

The process for inserting a shape is about the same as inserting a picture except for the fact that you have many more shape options to choose from compared to pictures.

For the most part, the types of shapes you can insert are fairly basic but good enough to get the job done in most cases. You can find the insert a shape button next to the insert pictures button. Figure 3.26 shows the various types of shapes that you can insert into your document.

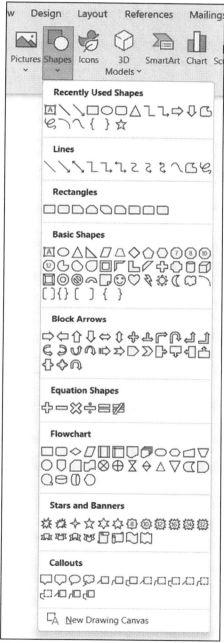

Figure 3.26

Once you select a shape from the list, you will not see anything change until you click and drag within your document to "draw" your shape. Once you let go of the mouse, you will have your shape on the page. You can then resize it by clicking on one of the round dots on the sides or corners until you see a double-sided arrow and then drag it to make it larger or smaller. You can also click on the rotate icon at the top of the image to rotate your shape in either direction. You will also notice that you have the same layout options icon that appears when you click on your shape to select it.

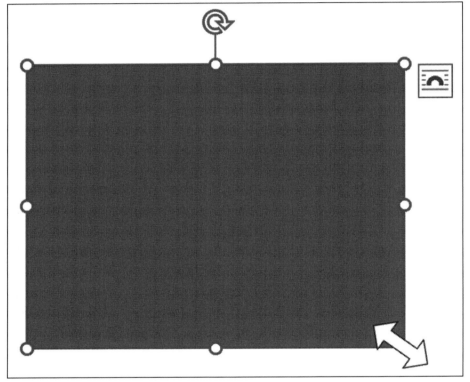

Figure 3.27

If you were to right click on your shape and choose *Format Shape*, you will then be given many options to do things such as change its color, remove the fill so it's just an outline, change the stroke (thickness) of the outline, add shadows, change its alignment and much more (figure 3.28).

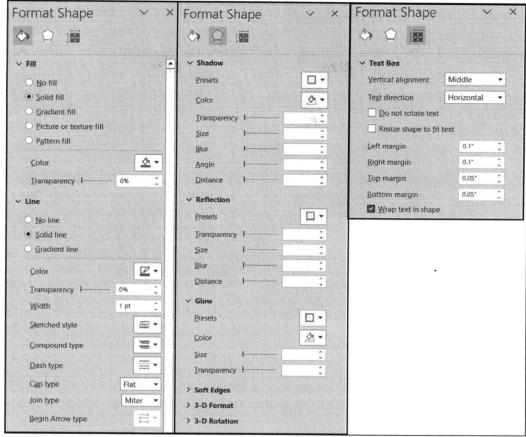

Figure 3.28

As an example, I have a graphic with food on some shelves and I will add various shapes to the graphic so you can see how it can be used. Once you add your shapes, you can move, delete or edit them as needed simply by selecting them.

Figure 3.29

Inserting Text Boxes

Normally when you type text into your document, it stays within the body of that document and outside of things such as pictures and shapes. But what if you need to add some text on top of a picture for example? Fortunately, that is very easy to do with the use of text boxes.

Text boxes are moveable boxes that contain text that you can edit just like any other text. There are a couple of ways to add them to your document based on the type of text box you need.

If you go to the *Insert* tab and then the *Text* group, you can click on *Text Box,* and it will show you all the different styles of text boxes you can insert into your document (figure 3.30). At the bottom of this menu, you will see an option that says Draw Text Box which can be used to create a basic text box anywhere on the page and is the option I prefer to use. You will also find this option under the Shapes section.

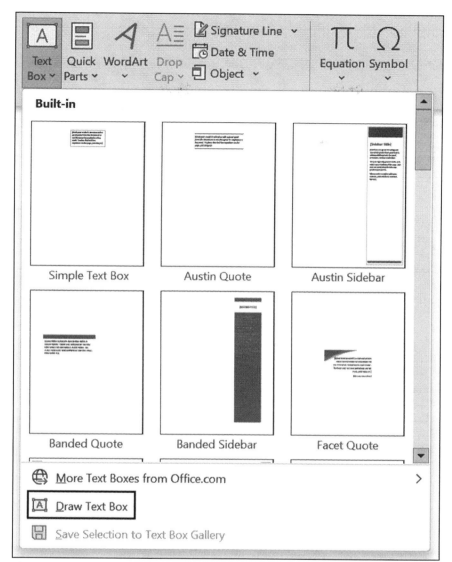

Figure 3.30

If you use one of the built-in text boxes, you might find that you need to change the layout option to *in front of text* before you can move it on top of your picture. If you use the *Draw Text Box* option, you can simply draw your box right on top of your picture.

When you first draw a text box, you will see that it has a white background and a black border. If you want to have only the text shown, you can right click the text box and choose the *No fill* and *No line* options (figure 3.32).

Figure 3.31

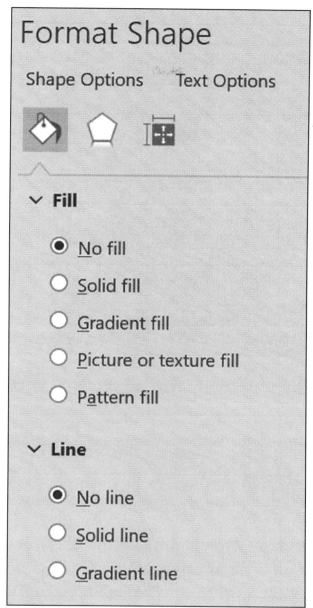

Figure 3.32

Figure 3.33 shows my text boxes after removing the fill and line and also changing the text color to white so it stands out against the background.

Figure 3.33

Drawing

I had discussed the Drawing tab in the last chapter but wanted to go into a little more detail in this chapter in case you thought you might have a need to use the tools within this tab.

Most people who use the drawing feature do so to make quick markups on their documents rather than try and create works of art with the basic tools provided here. As you can see in figure 3.34, the options are fairly limited when it comes to what kind of things you can do with these tools.

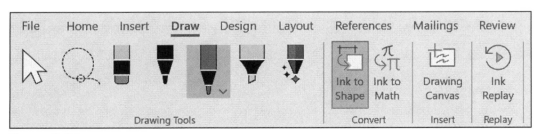

Figure 3.34

If you want to change the color or thickness of a pen, marker, or highlighter, simply click the down arrow next to it and choose a new color or click on one of the thickness settings to change the size of the pen tip.

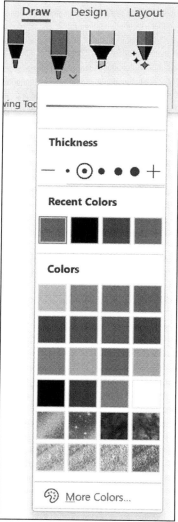

Figure 3.35

Figure 3.36 shows a floor plan that was marked up using the drawing tools. The tables at the upper right were highlighted using the highlighter tools and the tables in the center were crossed out using the pen tool and the arrow next to them was also drawn with the pen tool.

The arrow over to the right as well as the circles and rectangle at the bottom were created using the *Ink to Shape* tool. When you are using this tool, Word will try and figure out what you are intending to draw and then create a refined version of that shape after you let go of the mouse. It's not perfect and sometimes you will have to try it more than once to get the shape you are looking for. Just remember to use the undo option if you don't like the results!

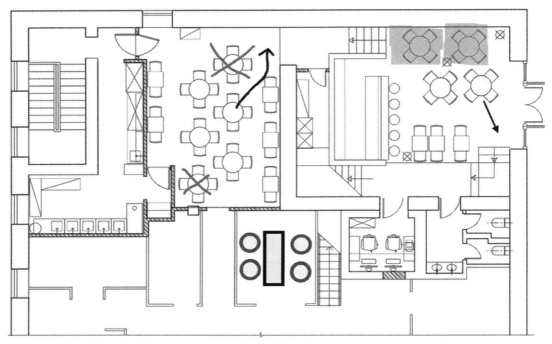

Figure 3.36

You can also use the eraser tool to remove a specific shape or drawing. The arrow tool is used to move your shapes around after you draw them. You can also use it to stretch, shrink or enlarge your drawn items.

Save vs. Save As

As you are working on your document, your changes are only being temporarily saved in the memory on your computer until you tell Word to actually save your work. This means if Word or your computer were to crash, you would lose any changes that were made since the last time you clicked on Save.

It is important to save your work every so often, especially after making some major changes because you don't want to get stuck having to redo all the work that was done since the last save in case your computer has a problem.

If you do have a crash, you might get lucky because Word has an auto recover feature that will try and restore your document to the state it was in when Word was shut down improperly. If Word is able to recover your document, it will prompt you to open and save it the next time you open Word.

If you look at the upper left corner of Word, you will see an *AutoSave* setting that may or may not be enabled. This will automatically save your document every ten minutes to your online OneDrive cloud storage account (discussed in chapter 7). This is fine unless you do not know how to access your OneDrive account to copy your document back to your actual computer if needed.

Figure 3.37

Next to AutoSave, you will find a picture of a floppy disk which is used as a quick way to save your work simply by clicking on it. Every time you click this icon, your work will be saved to your hard drive, and it will also overwrite any previous saves you have performed. If you like keyboard shortcuts, you can press **Ctrl-S** on your keyboard every time you want to save your document.

If you have the need to save your document with a different name or in a different location on your computer, you can use the *save as* feature to do this.

Let's say you were working on a brochure and wanted to keep a copy of the current version as is while still making additional changes to it. If you save the brochure with a different name such as Brochure v2 for example, you can have a file called **Brochure.docx** and also a file called **Brochure v2.docx** in the same folder.

Another option is to keep the original name and save a copy in a different folder on your computer. You can have two identical files with different names in the same folder but can't have two files with the same name in the same folder even if one was a completely different file.

To save a copy of your document with a different name or in a different location, you will need to use the save as option which can be found by clicking on the *File* tab and then on *Save As*.

To save your document in the **same** folder\location, you can simply type in a new name in the box at the upper right and click the *Save* button. To save your document with the same (or different) name in a different folder, you can either click on one of your recent folders shown on the right or click the *Browse* button over on the left.

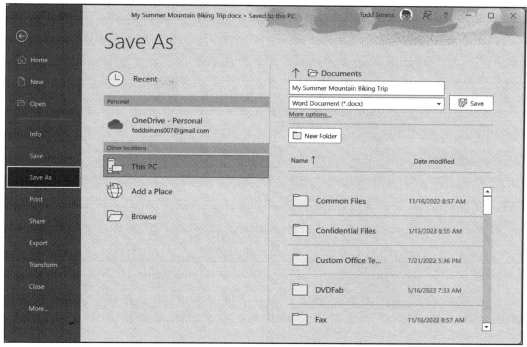

Figure 3.38

If you click on the Browse button, you can then browse your hard drive and choose the folder which you want to use to save your document in. You can then either keep the same file\document name or type in a new one in the *File name* box and then click the *Save* button (figure 3.39).

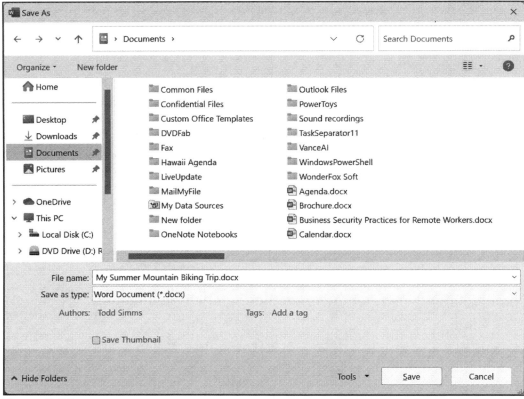

Figure 3.39

I have saved a copy of my document in a different folder (Bike Trip Info) but kept the name the same. Now when I go to the *Open* option in the File tab and look at my recent documents, I can see this new copy and the original and can open either one independently of the other and then any changes I make will be saved specifically to the one I have opened.

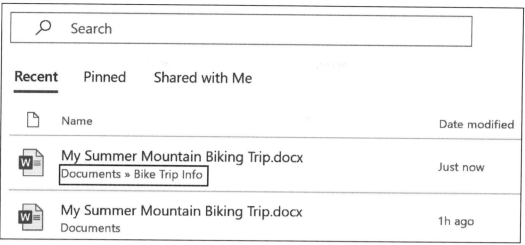

Figure 3.40

One advanced option related to saving I wanted to mention is that you have the ability to save your document as a different type of file other than a Word document. If you click on the arrow in the Save as type box, you will see all of the available file types that you can save your document as. This might come in handy someday if someone requests a different version of your file but it's unlikely it will ever happen!

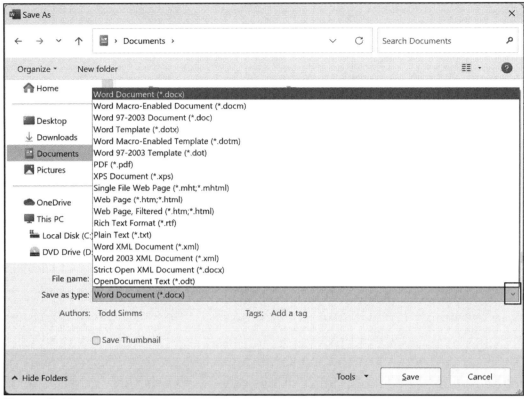

Figure 3.41

Speaking of files, I also wanted to take a moment to talk about file extensions. File extensions are the letters at the end of a file name after the period. If you look at figure 3.42, you will see several files with names such as Billing Info.xlsx and Brochure.docx. The file extensions for these two examples are **.xlsx** and **.docx**. File extensions are what tell your computer which program should be used to open the file. So, if you change the file extension by accident or on purpose, your computer won't know what program to use to open the file without you specifically telling it.

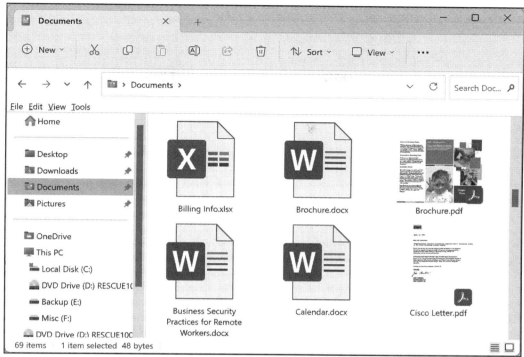

Figure 3.42

Changing the file extension to something your computer doesn't recognize will even change the file icon.

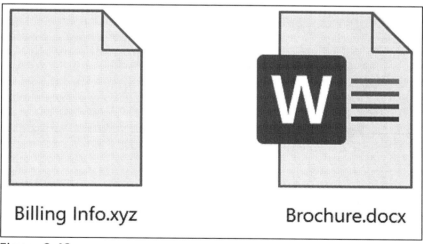

Figure 3.43

I realize this is more of an advanced topic but thought it would be worth mentioning.

Inserting Blank Pages and Page Breaks

As you work on your document, you will notice that Word will add pages as necessary, so you never have to worry about running out of room or adding additional pages manually.

Even though Word takes care of adding these new pages as needed, you might come across a situation where you will want to add a new page on your own.

Let's say you are writing a book and come to the end of the chapter and want to start on the next one. Most likely you will not start the next chapter on the same page as the last one and will want it to start on a new page.

This is where the Blank Page option comes in handy. To add a new blank page, simply put the cursor at the end of the text where you want the last page to end and go to the *Insert* tab and then click on *Blank Page* in the *Pages* group.

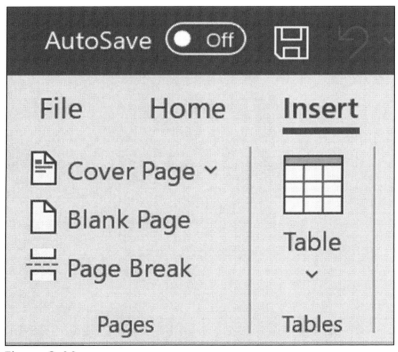

Figure 3.44

Word will then add a new blank page after your current page, and you can then continue working on your document on this new page. You can also use the new blank page tool to add a page in the middle of your document between two existing pages. Just be sure to place your cursor where you want the new blank page to start before doing so.

Page breaks are similar to blank pages but are used to add space between paragraphs by pushing the text below the page break to the next page rather than adding an entire new page.

If you look at figure 3.45, I want to have the paragraph that begins with the word Conclusion moved to the next page while leaving the paragraph that is before it where it is currently located.

To do this I can place my cursor after the word data in the top paragraph and then insert a page break to have the bottom paragraph moved down to the next page. You can see the results in figure 4.46.

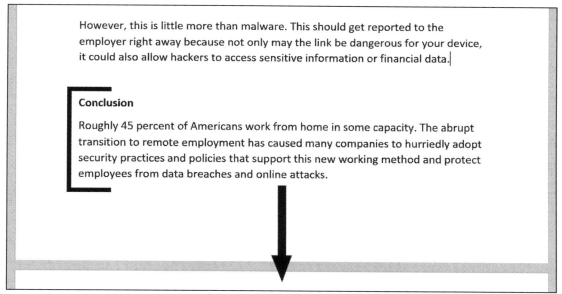

Figure 3.45

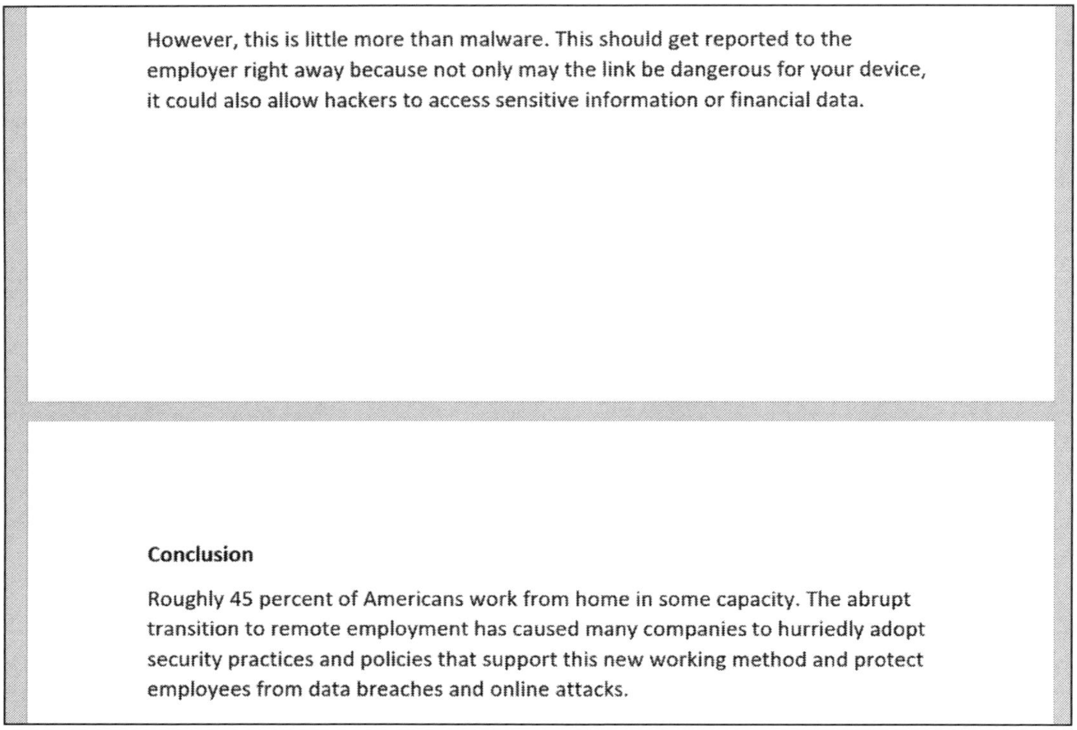

However, this is little more than malware. This should get reported to the employer right away because not only may the link be dangerous for your device, it could also allow hackers to access sensitive information or financial data.

Conclusion

Roughly 45 percent of Americans work from home in some capacity. The abrupt transition to remote employment has caused many companies to hurriedly adopt security practices and policies that support this new working method and protect employees from data breaches and online attacks.

Figure 3.46

Views (Zoom)

I mentioned the Zoom tool in the last chapter but wanted to take a little more time to go over this feature in more detail. When working with Word on your screen, it is important to have the view set so you can easily see what you are doing and also get an idea of how your page layout is looking as well.

When you go to the View tab and then the Zoom section, you will have a button labeled Zoom and then another one labeled 100% next to that. Clicking the 100% button will most likely zoom too far out to fit the entire page on your screen. Your results may vary depending on your monitor size and screen resolution.

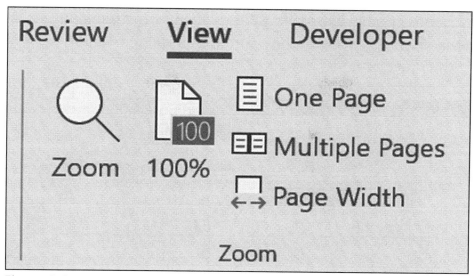

Figure 3.47

When you click on the Zoom button, you will be given several choices as to how you want to set your zoom level (figure 3.48). You can also type in an exact percentage if you like or go up or down in 1% increments using the arrow buttons.

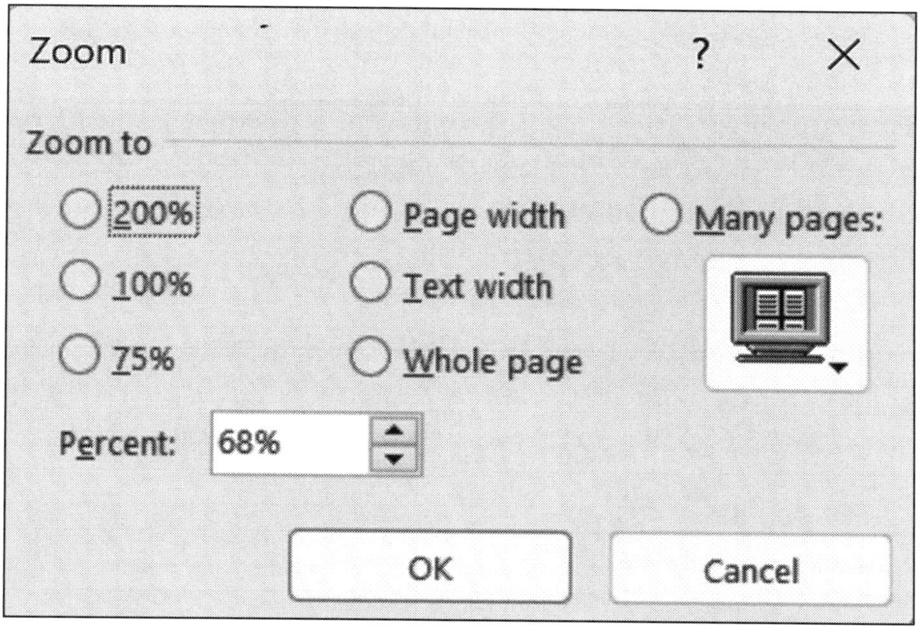

Figure 3.48

95

The *Many pages* choice will display all the pages in your document on the screen so you can imagine how small the pages would be if you had more than just three as shown below!

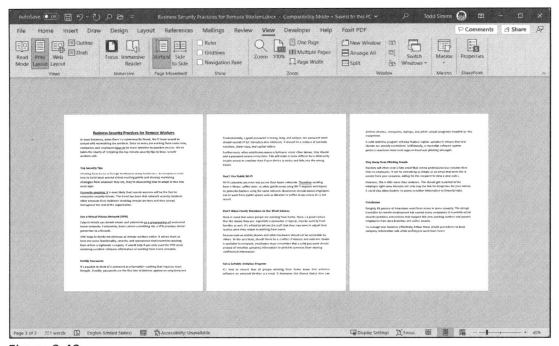

Figure 3.49

The *One Page* option from figure 3.47 will make a single page fit on the screen and the *Multiple Pages* option will try and fit as many pages as it can on the screen based on your zoom level. The more you are zoomed out, the more pages it will be able to fit on the screen.

Finally, the *Page Width* option will make the current page take up the width of the Word interface. This comes in handy when you are trying to make the page as large as you can while fitting it on the screen width wise.

Chapter 4 – Formatting

When working on your document in Word, you need to take into consideration how it is formatted because that will affect its overall appearance and how easy it is to read. If you have too many fonts and are using multiple colors and making every other word bold, then that won't make for a professional looking document.

Many people like to choose their fonts, sizes, colors and so on before starting the document while others like to format as they go along. And if you prefer to do your formatting as the last step then that is perfectly fine too.

Document formatting should not be a super involved process because less formatting often looks better than too much formatting. In this chapter, I will be showing you some ways to make your document stand out while still being easy to read.

Formatting Text
Since most of the content of your document will be text, it makes sense to have this text formatted nicely so it looks professional and is easy to read. One thing to consider when formatting the text within your document is consistency. If you use too many fonts or have certain text much larger than other text, you will notice that your document will start to look cluttered and unpleasant to the eye.

Figure 4.1 shows an open document with no formatting applied. It uses the default Calibri font set to size the 11-point size. It also uses the Normal style and the left justified paragraph setting.

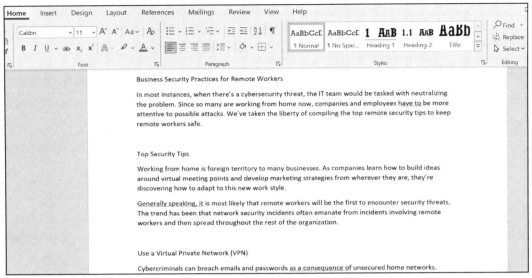

Figure 4.1

What I am going to do is make the paragraph headers bold and increase their font size to 14. I will the make set the paragraphs to be justified which means they will be flush with the margins on both the left and right sides.

Figure 4.2 shows the tools I will use to accomplish it. The B icon is used to make text bold, the box with the 11 in it is used to change the font size and the icon with the four equal lines is used to justify my paragraph style.

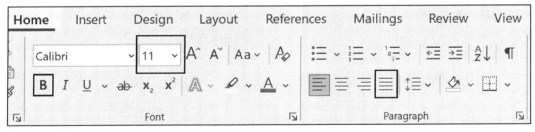

Figure 4.2

To make my paragraph headers bold and 14 point, I will need to highlight them first so Word knows what text to apply the formatting to. I can highlight them all or one at a time. To highlight a line of text, all I need to do is place the cursor at the beginning or end of the text and click, hold and drag until the text is selected. To highlight more than one line at a time, I can hold down the *Ctrl* key on the keyboard and then highlight the next line of text. Then I can set the text to bold and change the font size while it is highlighted rather than having to make one change, highlight the text again and then make the next change.

Business Security Practices for Remote Workers

In most instances, when there's a cybersecurity threat, the IT team would be tasked with neutralizing the problem. Since so many are working from home now, companies and employees have to be more attentive to possible attacks. We've taken the liberty of compiling the top remote security tips to keep remote workers safe.

Top Security Tips

Working from home is foreign territory to many businesses. As companies learn how to build ideas around virtual meeting points and develop marketing strategies from wherever they are, they're discovering how to adapt to this new work style.

Generally speaking, it is most likely that remote workers will be the first to encounter security threats. The trend has been that network security incidents often emanate from incidents involving remote workers and then spread throughout the rest of the organization.

Use a Virtual Private Network (VPN)

Cybercriminals can breach emails and passwords as a consequence of unsecured home networks.

Figure 4.3

Figure 4.4 shows the formatting results and as you can see, the text remains highlighted in case I want to make additional changes. To clear the highlighted text, all I need to do is click somewhere on the page with my mouse.

Business Security Practices for Remote Workers

In most instances, when there's a cybersecurity threat, the IT team would be tasked with neutralizing the problem. Since so many are working from home now, companies and employees have to be more attentive to possible attacks. We've taken the liberty of compiling the top remote security tips to keep remote workers safe.

Top Security Tips

Working from home is foreign territory to many businesses. As companies learn how to build ideas around virtual meeting points and develop marketing strategies from wherever they are, they're discovering how to adapt to this new work style.

Generally speaking, it is most likely that remote workers will be the first to encounter security threats. The trend has been that network security incidents often emanate from incidents involving remote workers and then spread throughout the rest of the organization.

Use a Virtual Private Network (VPN)

Cybercriminals can breach emails and passwords as a consequence of unsecured home networks.

Figure 4.4

I will now select all the text in my document to apply the paragraph formatting to. I can use my mouse to click, hold and drag down all the pages within my document or I can go to the *Editing* group on the *Home* tab and then click on the *Select* button and finally *Select All*.

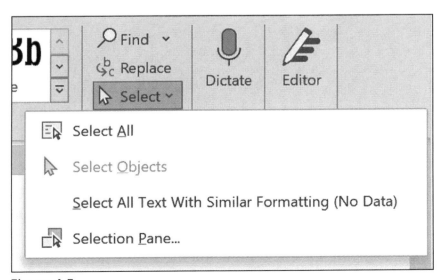

Figure 4.5

What I like to do for this situation is use the *Ctrl-A* keyboard shortcut (*Command-A* for Mac users) to have everything on the page selected. Once everything is selected, I will click on the *Justify* paragraph setting to have my text left and right justified to the margins. You will notice that the heading text stays to the left because it is a separate line of text and Word will not try and stretch it out to reach the right side of the page.

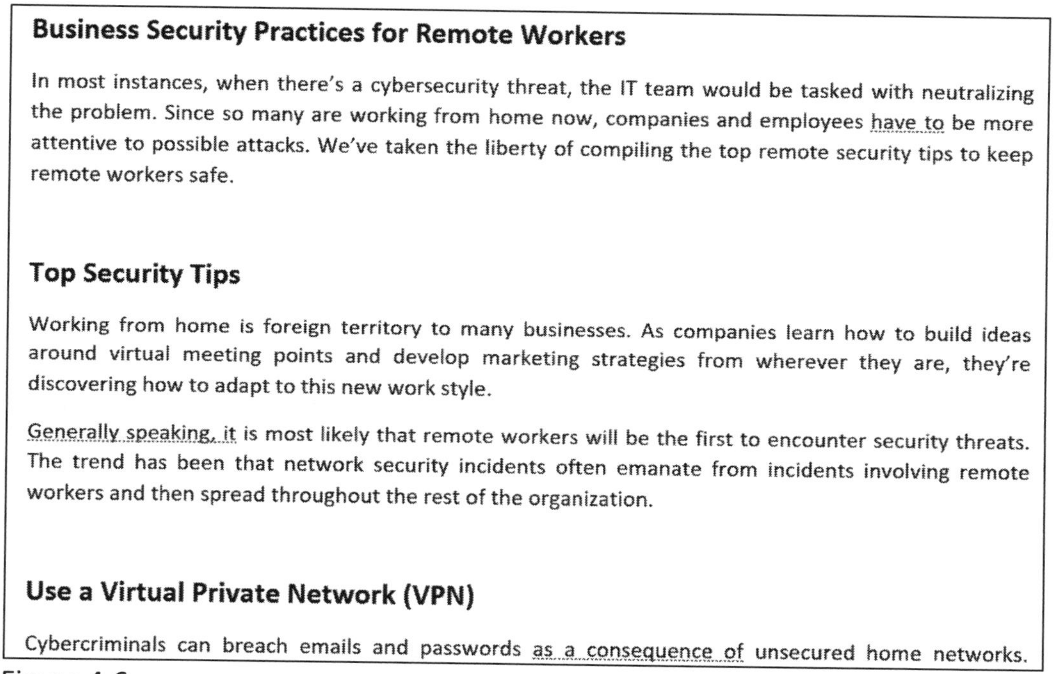

Business Security Practices for Remote Workers

In most instances, when there's a cybersecurity threat, the IT team would be tasked with neutralizing the problem. Since so many are working from home now, companies and employees have to be more attentive to possible attacks. We've taken the liberty of compiling the top remote security tips to keep remote workers safe.

Top Security Tips

Working from home is foreign territory to many businesses. As companies learn how to build ideas around virtual meeting points and develop marketing strategies from wherever they are, they're discovering how to adapt to this new work style.

Generally speaking, it is most likely that remote workers will be the first to encounter security threats. The trend has been that network security incidents often emanate from incidents involving remote workers and then spread throughout the rest of the organization.

Use a Virtual Private Network (VPN)

Cybercriminals can breach emails and passwords as a consequence of unsecured home networks.

Figure 4.6

If I change my mind and want to remove all the formatting I have done to my document or part of my document. I can select the text that I want to undo and then click on the *Clear All Formatting* button in the *Font* group on the *Home* tab as seen in figure 4.7.

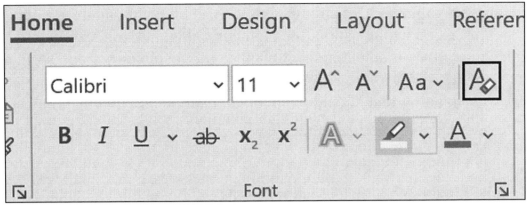

Figure 4.7

There are many more ways to format text besides what you have seen in my example, but I just wanted to show you how the process is done. You can play with the other formatting tools and try them out on the text that you highlight. Just remember that you can easily undo any changes you have made with the Undo button or the Ctrl-Z keyboard shortcut. One important tip is that you can hover the mouse over any of the icons on the Ribbon and it will tell you what that particular tool will do.

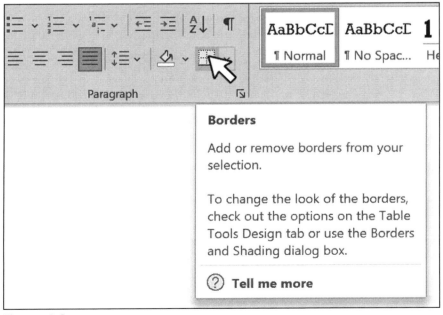

Figure 4.8

Changing Fonts and Sizes

In the last section on text formatting, I had changed the font to bold and also changed the font size in my document. In this section, I want to spend some time on fonts themselves. A font can be thought of as a style applied to text that has its own unique characteristics. Any time you read an article online or even in a book or magazine, you are most likely seeing many different fonts, or typestyles as they are also known.

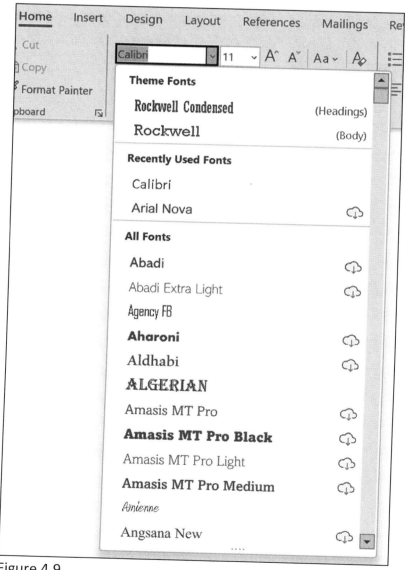

Figure 4.9

If you were to click on the font dropdown box in the Home tab, you will see all the fonts that are installed on your computer. Your computer will come with a selection of fonts when you buy it and when you install certain programs such as Word or Photoshop for example, they will most likely install some additional fonts on your computer. You can also buy fonts online as well as download many for free. You can even copy fonts from one computer to another if you know how to do so.

Figure 4.9 shows the fonts installed on my computer and your listing will most likely not look the same. Each font will have a preview of how the letters look if you were to use it in your document.

The fonts that have cloud icons next to them indicate that they are not installed on your computer but if you like them, you can install them simply by clicking on the cloud icon itself.

The section labeled *Recently Used Fonts* comes in handy because if there is a font that you use often, it will show up there making it easy to apply to some other text within your document.

To apply a font to your text, simply highlight that text and choose your font and it will then be applied to the text you highlighted as seen in Figure 4.10 after I apply the *Algerian* font to the bottom paragraph. Changing the font will not affect things like the text size, color or other formatting attributes such as bold, italics and underlined.

However, this is little more than malware. This should get reported to the employer right away because not only may the link be dangerous for your device, it could also allow hackers to access sensitive information or financial data.

CONCLUSION

ROUGHLY 45 PERCENT OF AMERICANS WORK FROM HOME IN SOME CAPACITY. THE ABRUPT TRANSITION TO REMOTE EMPLOYMENT HAS CAUSED MANY COMPANIES TO HURRIEDLY ADOPT SECURITY PRACTICES AND POLICIES THAT SUPPORT THIS NEW WORKING METHOD AND PROTECT EMPLOYEES FROM DATA BREACHES AND ONLINE ATTACKS.

Figure 4.10

To change the size of the font in use, you will need to select the text that you want this size change to apply to and then you can choose one of the default font sizes as seen in figure 4.11. If you want to type in your own custom size such as 15.5, you can do so as well. You can also see that the choices only go up to 72 but you can type in a larger number such as 150 manually if needed.

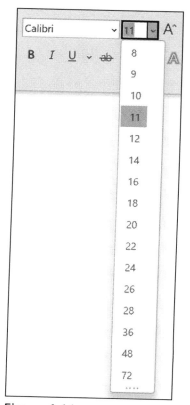

Figure 4.11

Creating Lists

Lists are a fairly common thing to use in Word so if you don't know what one is or how to use one then this section is for you! When you are adding text that works best in a list format, you can have Word create lists right from your text for you which will make the text easier to comprehend for your readers.

Figure 4.12 shows the ingredients for chocolate chip cookies and as you can see, it's just simple text with each ingredient on its own line.

Ingredients for chocolate chip cookies

Butter
Eggs
Vanilla
Baking soda
Water
Salt
Flour
Chocolate chips
Nuts (optional)

Figure 4.12

To create a list from this text, I will first need to highlight all of the ingredients and then go to the *Paragraph* group within the *Home* tab and choose which type of list I want to use. There are three main types of lists that you can use, and they are *bullets*, *numbering* and *multilevel*.

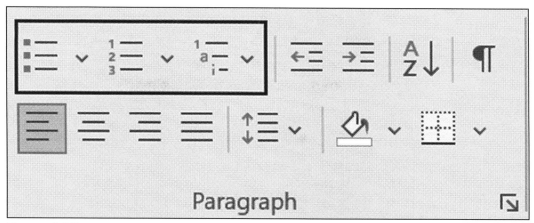

Figure 4.13

Something you might notice when you highlight text is that you will have a formatting box appear for a short amount of time that you can use to apply changes to your text as kind of a shortcut rather than having to find the specific setting in its usual location on the Ribbon (figure 4.14).

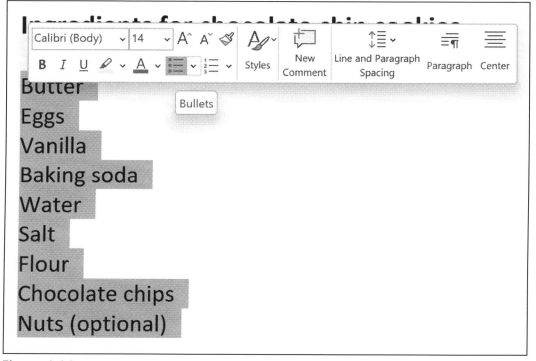

Figure 4.14

For my list, I will be using the bullet type and when I click the down arrow next to the list selection type, I can see that there are several styles of bullets to choose from. I will use the default black circle style. You can even create your own custom bullet style by clicking on *Define New Bullet*.

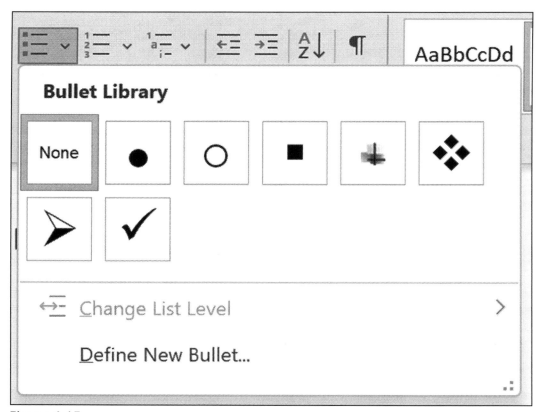

Figure 4.15

Figure 4.16 shows my list with the bullet style applied. You can see that it also indents the bulleted items to make them stand out even more. You can adjust this indent to move it more to the right or back to the left by using the increase or decrease indent buttons next to the list types in the same Paragraph section.

Ingredients for chocolate chip cookies

- Butter
- Eggs
- Vanilla
- Baking soda
- Water
- Salt
- Flour
- Chocolate chips
- Nuts (optional)

Figure 4.16

One thing to be aware of when creating lists is that when you press enter after one of the items in your list, Word will assume that you want whatever text you will be typing next to be part of the list so it will format it the same way. If this happens, you can simply highlight the text and click the list button again to have it removed.

Figure 4.17 shows an example of a numbered list. If you were to add a new item at the end or anywhere within the list, Word will update the list numbers so everything stays in order.

Ingredients for chocolate chip cookies

1. Butter
2. Eggs
3. Vanilla
4. Baking soda
5. Water
6. Salt
7. Flour
8. Chocolate chips
9. Nuts (optional)

Figure 4.17

Figure 4.18 shows the choices you have when creating a multilevel list. These are used when you have sub-levels or subcategories within your list.

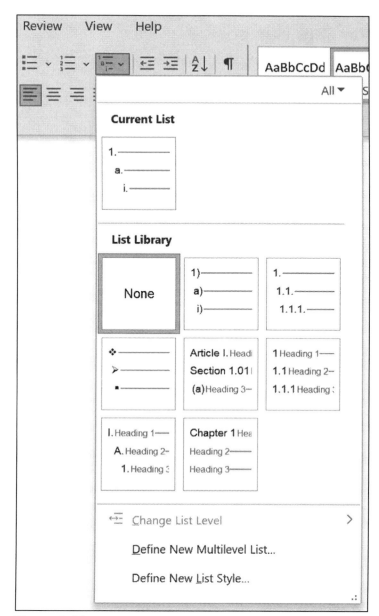

Figure 4.18

Figure 4.19 shows my chocolate chip cookie recipe list after adding these extra levels. Word will update the levels as you add new items to your list.

Ingredients for chocolate chip cookies

1) Butter
    a) 2 cups
2) Eggs
    a) 2
    b) Egg whites optional
3) Vanilla
    a) 1 tsp
4) Baking soda
    a) 1tsp
5) Water
    a) 2 cups
    b) Or 2 cups milk
6) Salt
    a) 1 tsp
7) Flour
    a) 2 cups
8) Chocolate chips
    a) 2 cups
    b) Or 2 cups peanut butter chips
9) Nuts (optional)

Figure 4.19

WordArt

Word has a nice feature called Word Art that lets you turn your plain text into something a bit more exciting by adding custom colors and effects to the text. This is different than simply changing the color or making it bold because it transforms it into an image that you can then customize to your liking.

For my example, I will type **Suzie's Graduation** into my document and then go to the *Insert* tab and to the *Text* group and select *WordArt*.

There are several styles to choose from with different colors, outlines, bevels and shadow effects. I will choose the blue style with a 3D look to it.

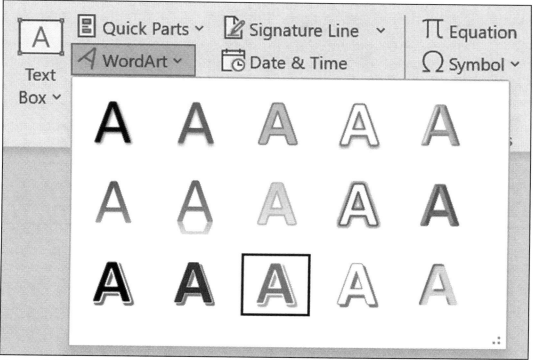

Figure 4.20

As you can see in figure 4.21, my simple text now changes to match my selection.

Suzie's Graduation!

Figure 4.21

Even though my text has been transformed into WordArt, I can still edit it or add to it if needed. If I were to click on it so there is a box around it like you would see for a picture, I will then be shown the *Shape Format* tab with many different groups that contain tools to further edit my new Word Art.

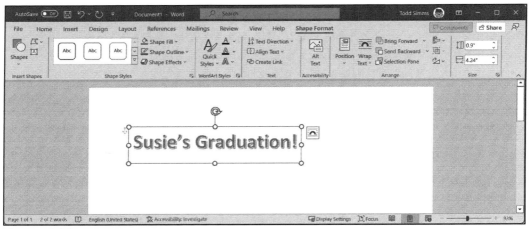

Figure 4.22

For example, if I were to click on the *Text Effects* icon under the *WordArt* Styles group, I would be shown many different types of effects that I can then apply to my text. Just keep in mind that these can only be used on text that has been transformed into WordArt and not regular text.

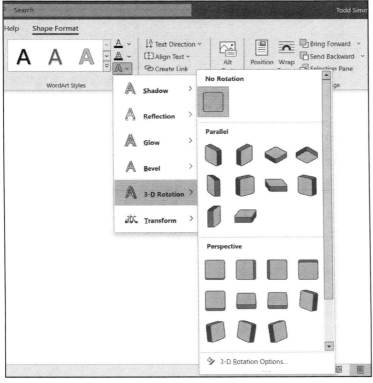

Figure 4.23

114

WordArt can be treated like text since you can edit it, but it can also be treated like a picture because you can click on the Layout Options icon to change its positioning such as being in front of normal text, or you can have text wrap around your WordArt.

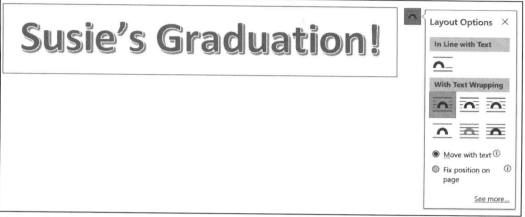

Figure 4.24

Page Colors and Borders

Another way to spruce up your document is to add page colors or backgrounds or even page borders. These enhancements are often used for things such as flyers or posters rather than letters or resumes for example.

If you go to the *Design* tab and then the *Page Background* group, you will see that you can add watermarks which I have discussed already as well as page colors and page borders.

If you click on *Page Color*, you will see that you can choose a variety of themes and colors as well as create your own color by clicking on *More colors*. If you choose an option under *Theme Colors*, it will change the background color of your document and might change the text color as well. For example, if you chose a dark theme, it will change the text to white so it is still readable.

115

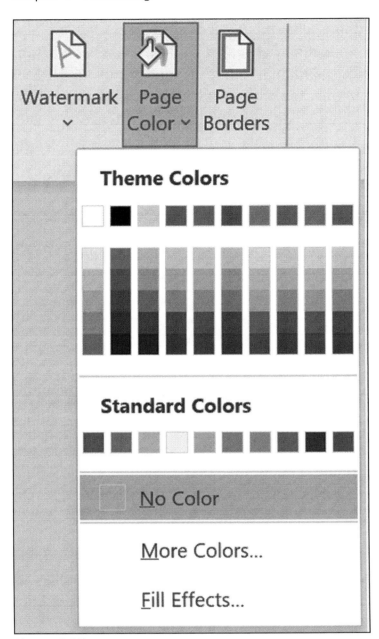

Figure 4.25

Clicking on *Fill Effects* will bring up some other background options such as adding a gradient, texture, pattern or background picture to your document.

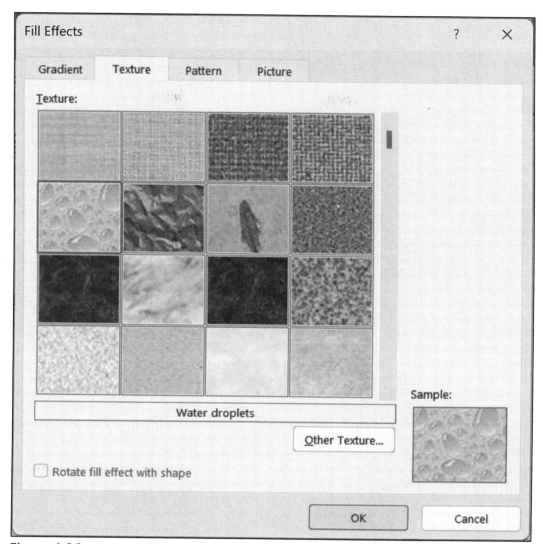

Figure 4.26

If I were to choose the water droplet texture and apply it to my document, I would get the results shown in figure 4.27. If I want to remove the background, I can simply go back to the Page Color dropdown menu and choose *No Color*. Keep in mind that if you plan to print your document with a page background, it will print the background as well and use a lot of ink if the *Print background colors and images* option is enabled which shouldn't be by default.

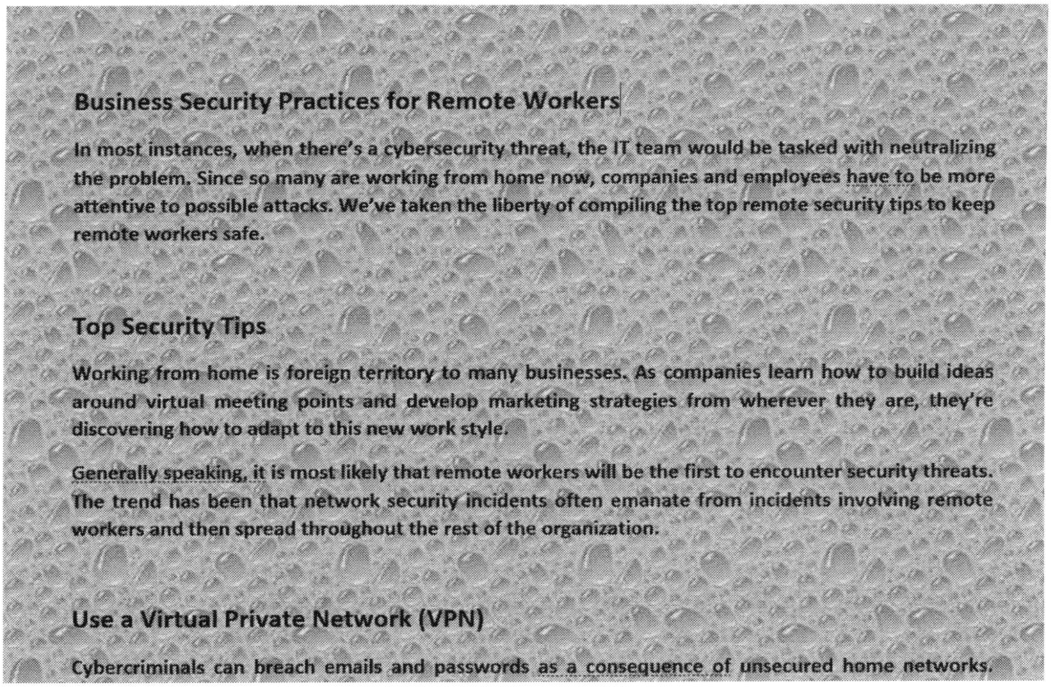

Business Security Practices for Remote Workers

In most instances, when there's a cybersecurity threat, the IT team would be tasked with neutralizing the problem. Since so many are working from home now, companies and employees have to be more attentive to possible attacks. We've taken the liberty of compiling the top remote security tips to keep remote workers safe.

Top Security Tips

Working from home is foreign territory to many businesses. As companies learn how to build ideas around virtual meeting points and develop marketing strategies from wherever they are, they're discovering how to adapt to this new work style.

Generally speaking, it is most likely that remote workers will be the first to encounter security threats. The trend has been that network security incidents often emanate from incidents involving remote workers and then spread throughout the rest of the organization.

Use a Virtual Private Network (VPN)

Cybercriminals can breach emails and passwords as a consequence of unsecured home networks.

Figure 4.27

Another way to make your document stand out is to add a border to a paragraph, page, or every page in your document. Figure 4.28 shows the options for borders and shading. You will have different selections based on which tab you choose. Once you pick a setting, you can then adjust the line style, color and thickness or even use some artwork for a border rather than a simple line.

You can then choose to apply it to the current page or the entire document. When you are on the first tab labeled *Borders*, you can apply a border to just a paragraph by highlighting the paragraph that you want to apply it to first.

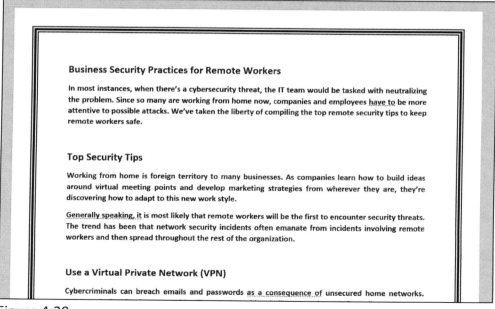

Figure 4.28

Figure 4.29 shows a simple page border while figure 4.30 shows a paragraph border added to the second paragraph on the page.

Business Security Practices for Remote Workers

In most instances, when there's a cybersecurity threat, the IT team would be tasked with neutralizing the problem. Since so many are working from home now, companies and employees have to be more attentive to possible attacks. We've taken the liberty of compiling the top remote security tips to keep remote workers safe.

Top Security Tips

Working from home is foreign territory to many businesses. As companies learn how to build ideas around virtual meeting points and develop marketing strategies from wherever they are, they're discovering how to adapt to this new work style.

Generally speaking, it is most likely that remote workers will be the first to encounter security threats. The trend has been that network security incidents often emanate from incidents involving remote workers and then spread throughout the rest of the organization.

Use a Virtual Private Network (VPN)

Cybercriminals can breach emails and passwords as a consequence of unsecured home networks.

Figure 4.29

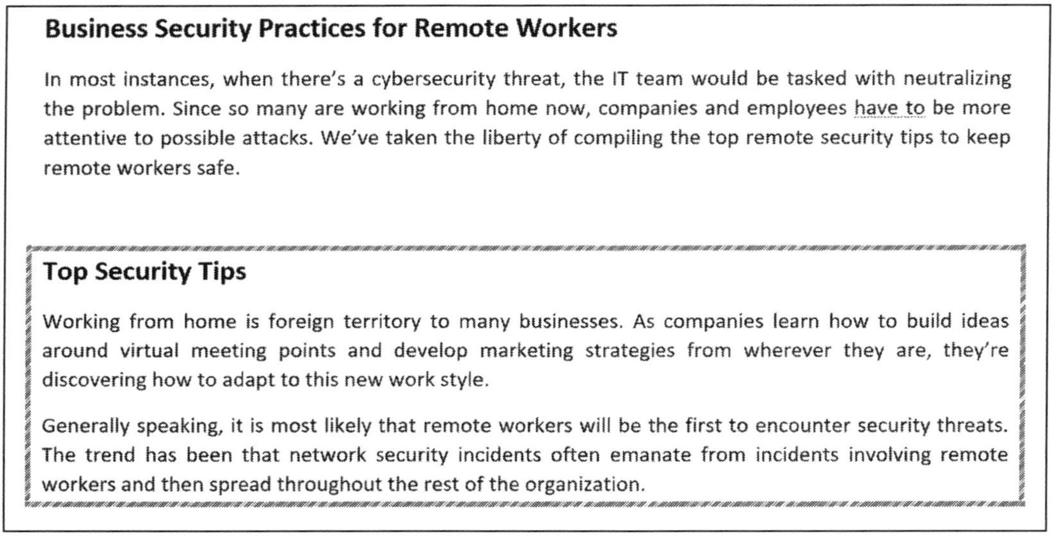

Business Security Practices for Remote Workers

In most instances, when there's a cybersecurity threat, the IT team would be tasked with neutralizing the problem. Since so many are working from home now, companies and employees have to be more attentive to possible attacks. We've taken the liberty of compiling the top remote security tips to keep remote workers safe.

Top Security Tips

Working from home is foreign territory to many businesses. As companies learn how to build ideas around virtual meeting points and develop marketing strategies from wherever they are, they're discovering how to adapt to this new work style.

Generally speaking, it is most likely that remote workers will be the first to encounter security threats. The trend has been that network security incidents often emanate from incidents involving remote workers and then spread throughout the rest of the organization.

Figure 4.30

Paragraph Justification

One simple way to alter the overall look of your document is by changing the way the text and paragraphs are justified on the page. By default, Word uses the left alignment setting for documents but as you can see in figure 4.31, the text on the right side of the page is uneven compared to the left side.

Business Security Practices for Remote Workers

In most instances, when there's a cybersecurity threat, the IT team would be tasked with neutralizing the problem. Since so many are working from home now, companies and employees have to be more attentive to possible attacks. We've taken the liberty of compiling the top remote security tips to keep remote workers safe.

Top Security Tips

Working from home is foreign territory to many businesses. As companies learn how to build ideas around virtual meeting points and develop marketing strategies from wherever they are, they're discovering how to adapt to this new work style.

Generally speaking, it is most likely that remote workers will be the first to encounter security threats. The trend has been that network security incidents often emanate from incidents involving remote workers and then spread throughout the rest of the organization.

Use a Virtual Private Network (VPN)

Cybercriminals can breach emails and passwords as a consequence of unsecured home networks. Fortunately, here's where something like a VPN provides similar protection to a firewall.

VPN helps to fortify the defenses of remote workers online. It allows them to have the same functionality, security, and appearance that resembles working from within a legitimate company. It would help if you only

Figure 4.31

If you would like to use a different setting, you can go to the *Home* tab and then the *Paragraph* group and choose either centered, right justified, or page justified.

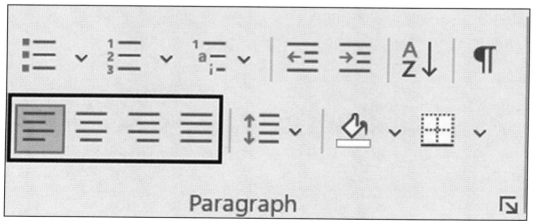

Figure 4.32

I will use the page justified option so the text on both the left and right sides of the page will be justified (even) with the margins. I will also use the centered option on the first line of the document and the results are shown in figure 4.33.

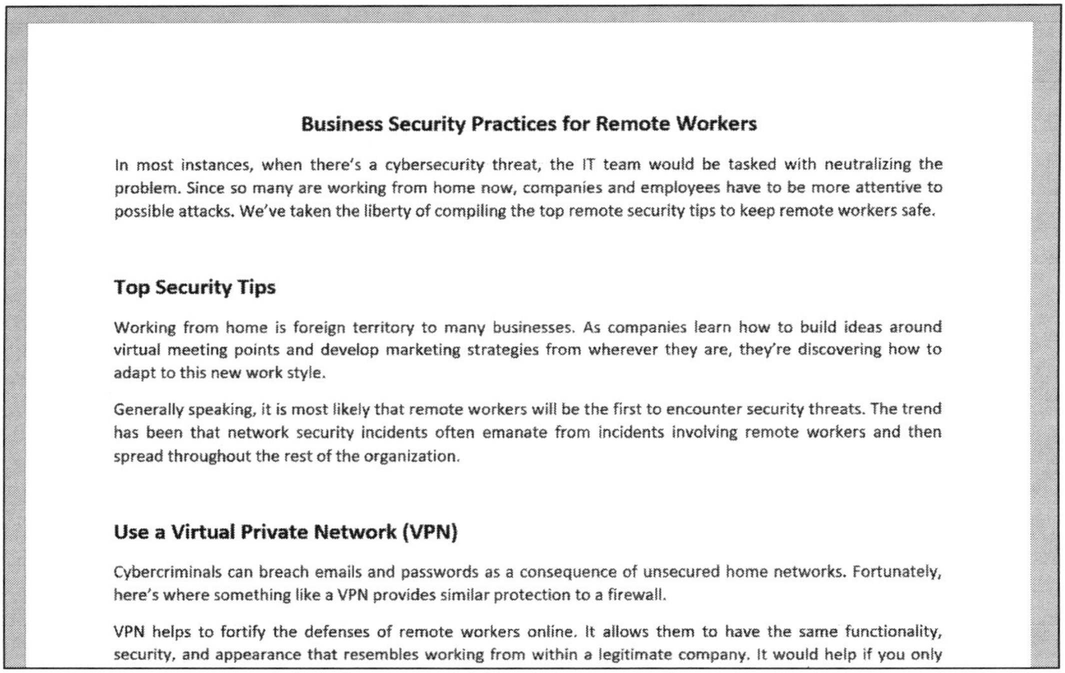

Business Security Practices for Remote Workers

In most instances, when there's a cybersecurity threat, the IT team would be tasked with neutralizing the problem. Since so many are working from home now, companies and employees have to be more attentive to possible attacks. We've taken the liberty of compiling the top remote security tips to keep remote workers safe.

Top Security Tips

Working from home is foreign territory to many businesses. As companies learn how to build ideas around virtual meeting points and develop marketing strategies from wherever they are, they're discovering how to adapt to this new work style.

Generally speaking, it is most likely that remote workers will be the first to encounter security threats. The trend has been that network security incidents often emanate from incidents involving remote workers and then spread throughout the rest of the organization.

Use a Virtual Private Network (VPN)

Cybercriminals can breach emails and passwords as a consequence of unsecured home networks. Fortunately, here's where something like a VPN provides similar protection to a firewall.

VPN helps to fortify the defenses of remote workers online. It allows them to have the same functionality, security, and appearance that resembles working from within a legitimate company. It would help if you only

Figure 4.33

Just remember to highlight the text you want this change to apply to, otherwise it will just be applied to whichever paragraph the cursor happens to be on.

Adding Page Numbers

If you need to number the pages within your document, it's a fairly easy process and you can also choose where the page numbers will go on the page.

The first thing you need to do is go to the *Insert* tab and then the *Header & Footer* section and choose *Page Number*. Then you will be able to choose where on the page you would like to place your page numbers and be shown a preview of how they will look (figure 4.34).

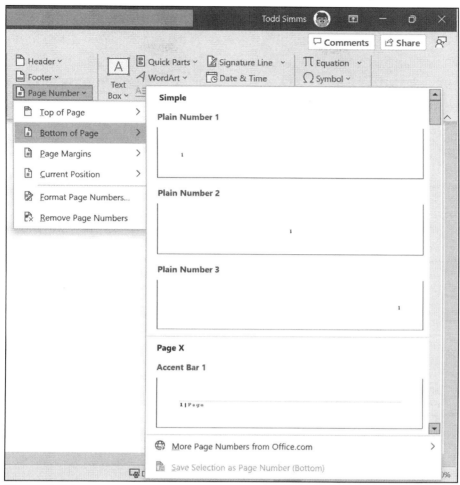

Figure 4.34

Once the page numbers are added, the footer (bottom) section of the page will be active in case you want to change the size, font, or color associated with your page number.

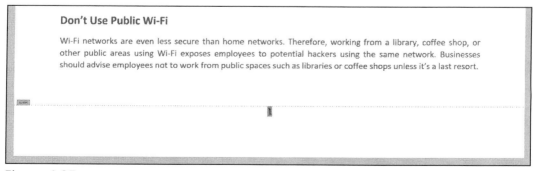

Figure 4.35

Up in the ribbon, you will have some checkboxes that you can use to change how your pages are numbered. The checkbox that says *Different First Page* is used if you want your page numbers to start on the second page. This comes in handy if you have a title page for your first page and the main content starts on the second page. The *Different Odd & Even Pages* checkbox is used to have different style page numbers on odd pages compared to even pages.

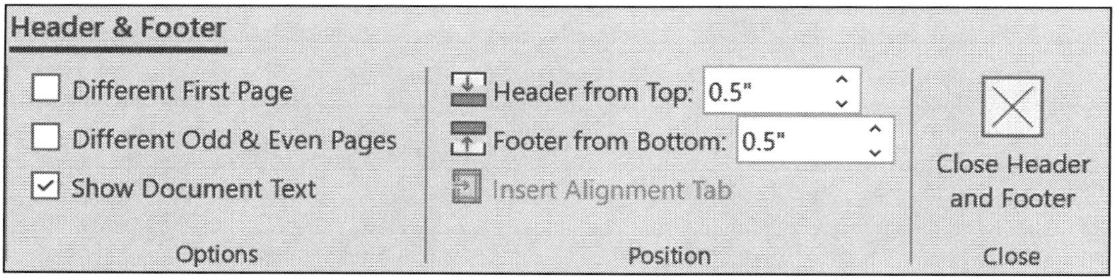

Figure 4.36

Once you have your page numbers configured, you can click on the *Close Header and Footer* button to go back to edit mode for your document. As you add more pages to your document either manually or automatically as you type, the next page numbers will be added at the same time.

Headers and Footers

Inserting a header or footer is similar to adding page numbers but you can use them to add useful information such as chapter names or reference notes etc. When you click on header or footer, you will have many styles to choose from as seen in figure 4.7.

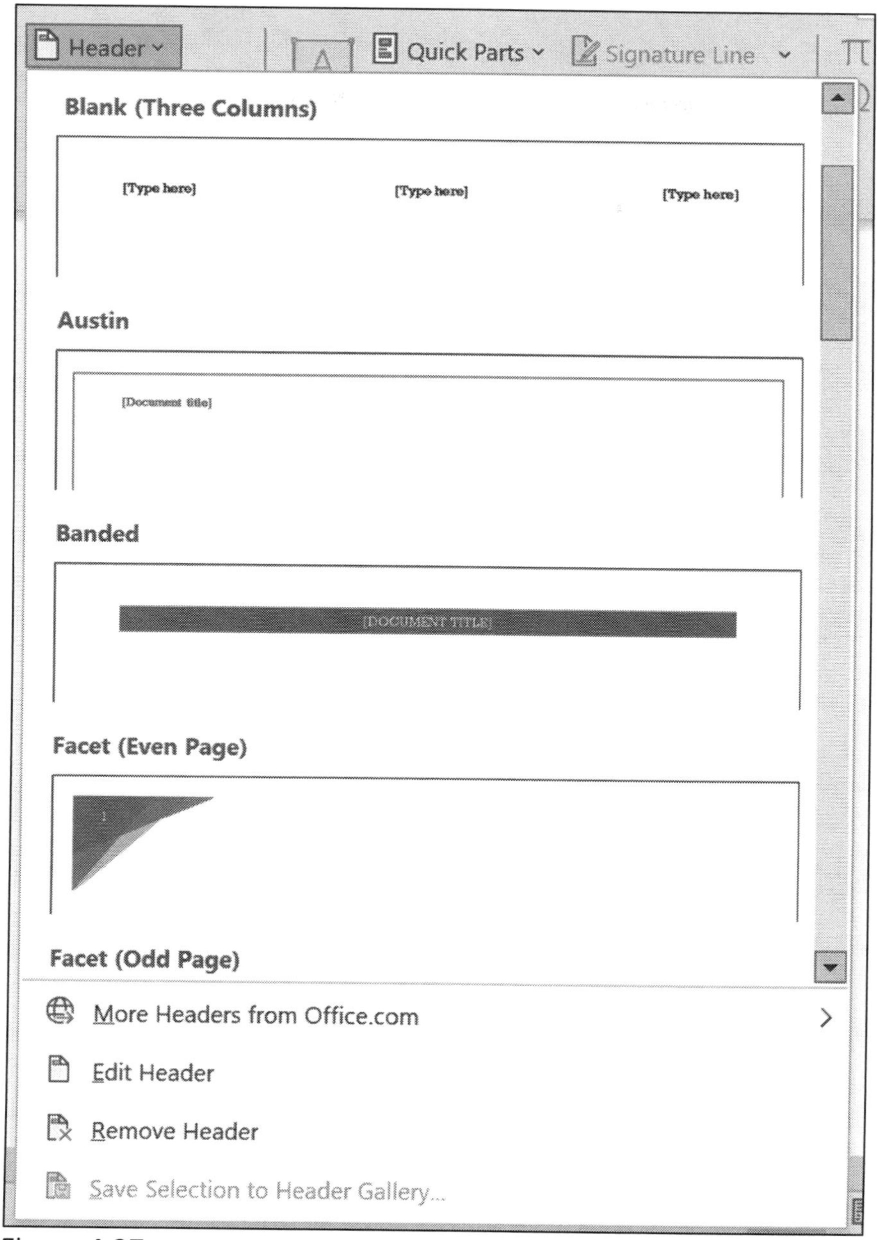

Figure 4.37

Figure 4.38 shows my document with a header style selected and then I was able to add my own custom text to the header. One thing you will notice is that your headers, footers and page numbers will appear lighter than the rest of your document. This is just to show you that they are headers and footers and when you print the document, they will print without being lighter in color.

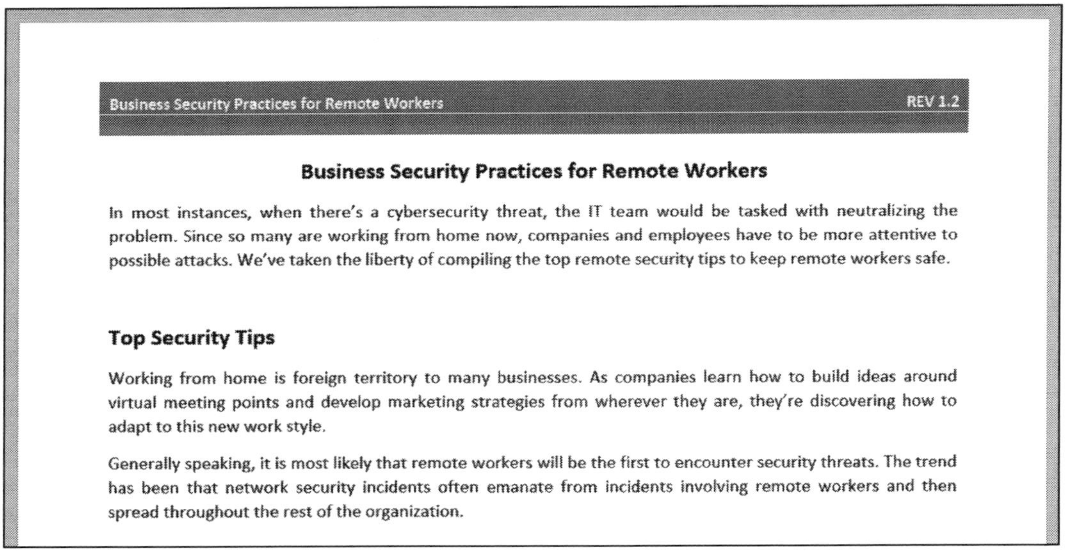

Business Security Practices for Remote Workers REV 1.2

Business Security Practices for Remote Workers

In most instances, when there's a cybersecurity threat, the IT team would be tasked with neutralizing the problem. Since so many are working from home now, companies and employees have to be more attentive to possible attacks. We've taken the liberty of compiling the top remote security tips to keep remote workers safe.

Top Security Tips

Working from home is foreign territory to many businesses. As companies learn how to build ideas around virtual meeting points and develop marketing strategies from wherever they are, they're discovering how to adapt to this new work style.

Generally speaking, it is most likely that remote workers will be the first to encounter security threats. The trend has been that network security incidents often emanate from incidents involving remote workers and then spread throughout the rest of the organization.

Figure 4.38

Chapter 5 – Reviewing Your Document

There is more to making your document easy to read besides proper formatting. If your document is full of spelling and grammar mistakes, your readers will find it harder to follow and might even end up a bit confused!

Grammar and Spell Checker (Editor)

You probably noticed that Word will mark spelling and grammar mistakes with red and blue squiggly underlines with red for spelling and blue for grammar. Figure 5.1 shows an example of a document with some spelling and grammar errors.

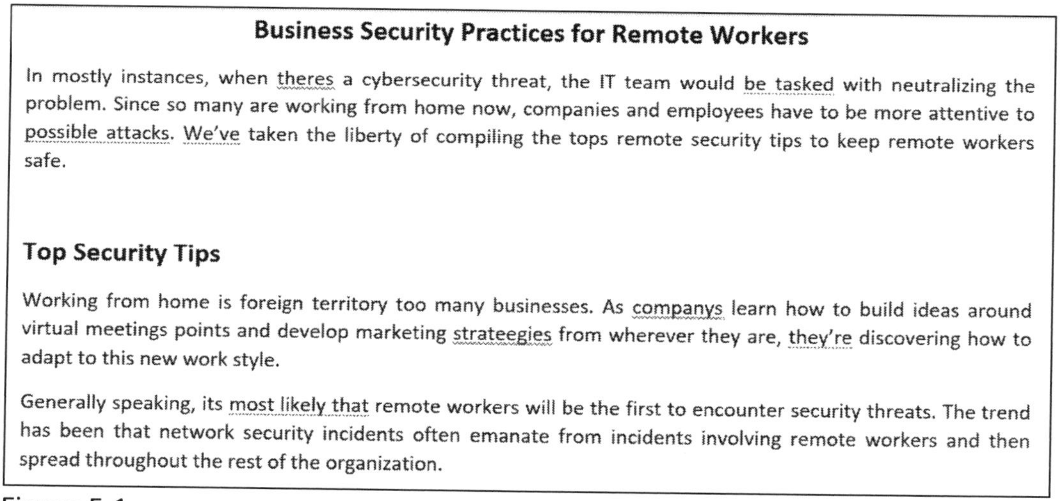

Business Security Practices for Remote Workers

In mostly instances, when theres a cybersecurity threat, the IT team would be tasked with neutralizing the problem. Since so many are working from home now, companies and employees have to be more attentive to possible attacks. We've taken the liberty of compiling the tops remote security tips to keep remote workers safe.

Top Security Tips

Working from home is foreign territory too many businesses. As companys learn how to build ideas around virtual meetings points and develop marketing strateegies from wherever they are, they're discovering how to adapt to this new work style.

Generally speaking, its most likely that remote workers will be the first to encounter security threats. The trend has been that network security incidents often emanate from incidents involving remote workers and then spread throughout the rest of the organization.

Figure 5.1

If you are the type who likes to fix spelling and grammar errors as you go along, you can right click on any of the underlined words and get suggestions for fixing the error (figure 5.2). If you find the suggestion that you want to use, you can simply click on it to have the change applied to your document.

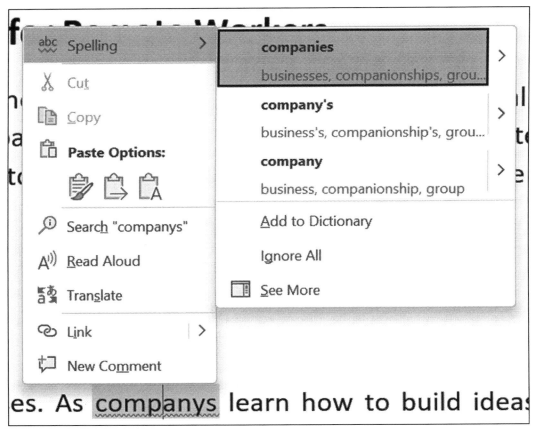

Figure 5.2

If you would rather check and fix all your spelling and grammar errors at once or when you are finished with your document, you can use the *Editor* feature to do so. The Editor can be found in the *Home* tab as well as in the *Review* tab.

The Editor will not only check for spelling and grammar mistakes but can also check for other corrections such as clarity, conciseness, punctuation and vocabulary.

When you first open the Editor, you will be shown your overall score regarding how well written your document is. You will also be shown how many of each type of correction might be needed. I say might because sometimes Word may suggest a change that might not be exactly correct, and you may like your version better.

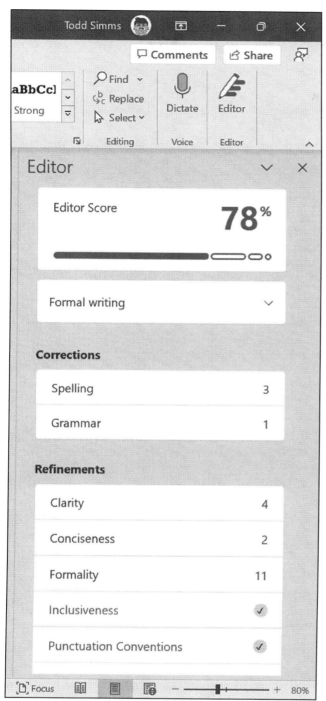

Figure 5.3

To view the corrections that the Editor has found, you can click on that specific category such as Spelling and go through each item one at a time as seen in figure 5.4.

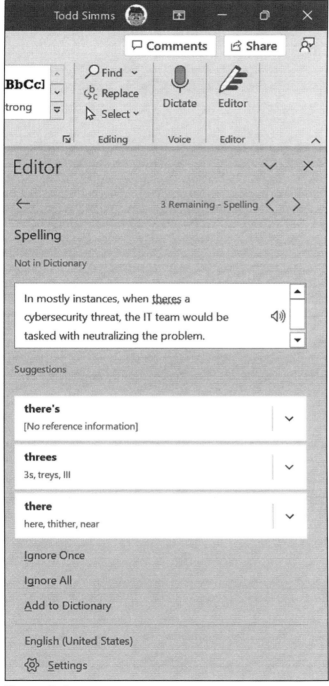

Figure 5.4

When you get to each item that needs attention, you can either choose from the suggestions or tell Word to ignore this instance or all instances if you do not want any corrections to be made. If it's a non-standard word that you will be using in the future, you can have Word add it to the dictionary so it won't mark it as incorrect in the future. If none of the suggestions fit but you know how to fix the mistake, then you can do so manually by going back to the document itself and making the change.

Navigation Pane

One handy feature that you can access from the View tab in Word is called the Navigation Pane and it can be used to help you make sure your document is organized properly and also help you find what you are looking for.

When you check the box next to Navigation Pane in the *Show* group, you will see that it is broken down into three different sections. The *Headings* section will show you any text that you have marked with an outline level which is used when creating a table of contents.

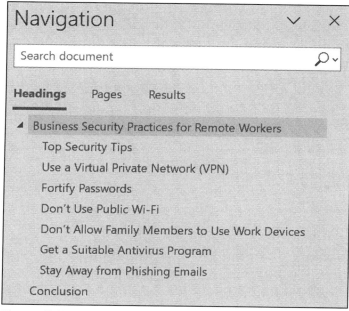

Figure 5.5

Even though this topic is beyond the scope of this book I will quickly show you how you set outline levels. Once you highlight the text you want to have in your table of contents, you can right click it and choose *Paragraph*. Then you can choose the outline level starting at level 1. Body Text is the default setting for all the text that is not part of your outline or table of contents. If you look back at figure 5.5, the first sentence "Business Security Practices for Remote Workers" is set to level 1 and the others are set to level 2 and that is why they are shown as sub-levels. The Conclusion line is also set to level 1.

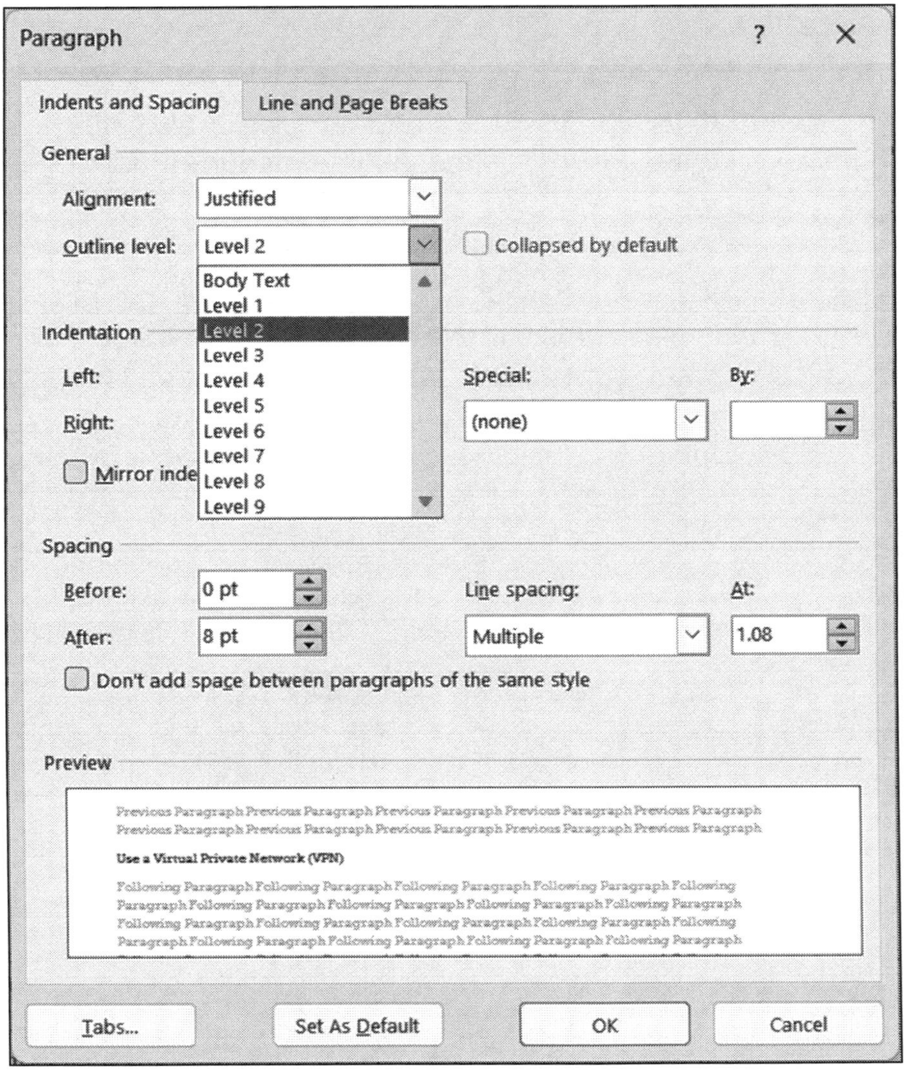

Figure 5.6

The *Pages* section will show you a thumbnail view of the pages in your document. You can use this to get a bird's eye view of your work and then you can click on any thumbnail image to be taken to that page.

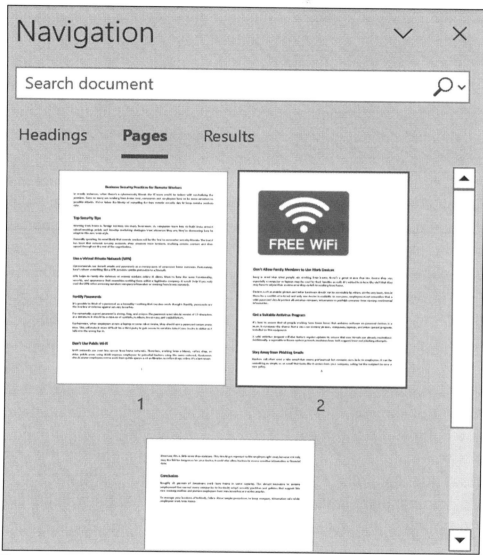

Figure 5.7

The *Results* section is used to display search results when you type in a word or phrase in the search box above. You can then click on any of the results to be taken directly to that word or phrase within your document.

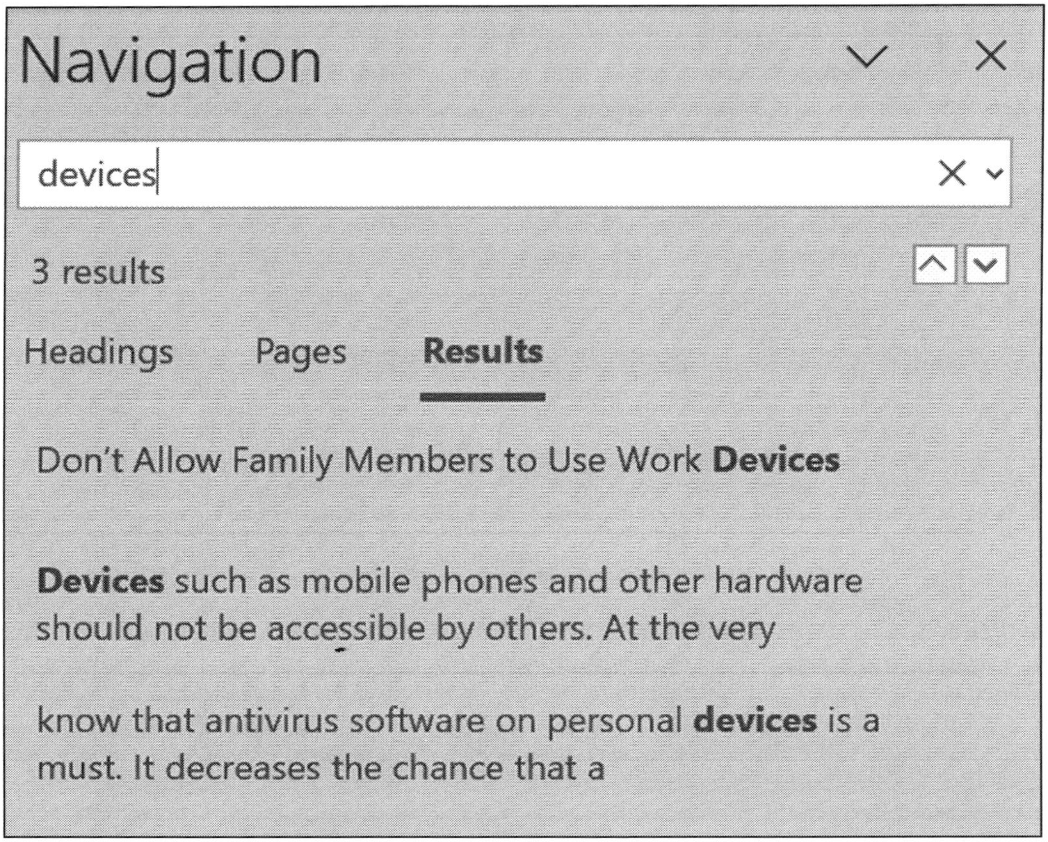

Navigation

devices

3 results

Headings   Pages   **Results**

Don't Allow Family Members to Use Work **Devices**

Devices such as mobile phones and other hardware should not be accessible by others. At the very

know that antivirus software on personal **devices** is a must. It decreases the chance that a

Figure 5.8

Grammarly Add-in

Overall, the Word Editor does a good job of showing what mistakes you have made and suggesting other changes to help your writing be as fluent as possible. But if you are the type who likes a second opinion on things, you can install the Grammarly spelling and grammar checker for Word and have it check out your document as well.

Add-ins are extra software that you can install on your computer that adds additional functionality to Word. For example, you can install add-ins that can electronically sign documents for you or give you a way to use additional clip art or pictures within your document. This might be more of an advanced topic so don't be afraid to ask your local geek for help with this process.

To view your installed add-ins, you can go to the *Insert* tab and then to the *Add-ins* section and then click on *My Add-ins*.

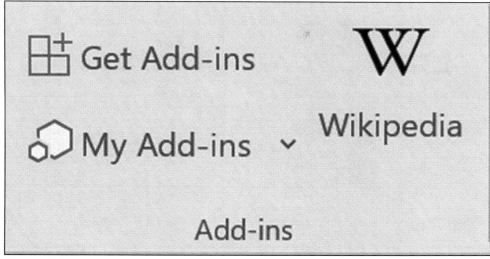

Figure 5.9

If you have not installed any add-ins, you will see a message similar to figure 5.10 and you can click on the *Office Store* button to see what types of add-ins are available to you.

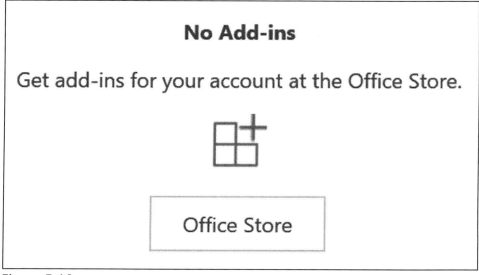

Figure 5.10

Add-ins are broken down into various categories and unfortunately the Grammarly add-in is not listed here, and you will not find it even if you search for it (as of this writing).

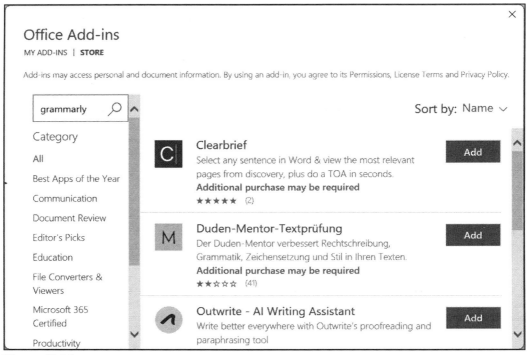

Figure 5.11

To get the Grammarly add-in for Word, you will have to go to their website and download it. It can be found at the following website address, or you can simply do a search for it with your web browser (figure 5.12).

https://www.grammarly.com/office-addin

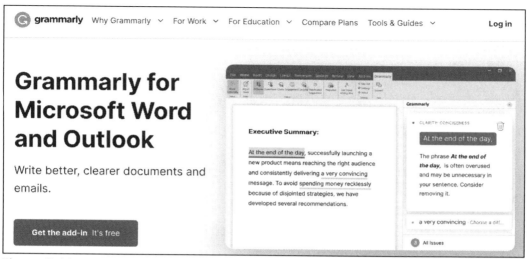

Figure 5.12

Once you download the software, you will have the option to install it for Word and Outlook or just Word if you do not want to use it with Outlook or if you do not use Outlook for your email.

After the installation is complete, you will have a Grammarly icon on your Home tab that you can click on at any time to open the Grammarly add-on.

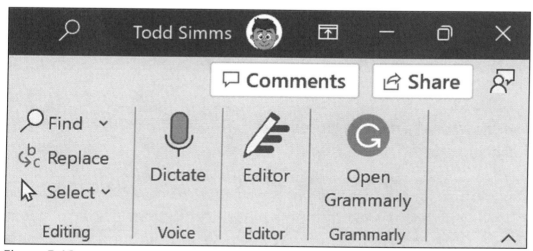

Figure 5.13

To use Grammarly, you will need to create a free account so you can log into it to use the add-in. If you do not have an account, you will be able to create one when you use it the first time.

After you are logged in, you can start the add-on and it will open a pane to the right of your document and show you the mistakes it has found as you scroll down the page. You can click on the suggested fix to have your document updated or you can ignore it and move on to the next one.

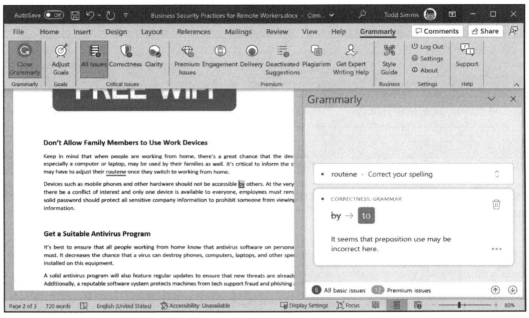

Figure 5.14

You can also click on the ellipses next to the suggestion to find out why it is being marked as incorrect.

You will also have additional options in your new Grammarly tab such as having all issues shown or only having corrections or clarity issues shown. Once you are finished with the add-on, you can simply close it by clicking on the X at the upper right or by clicking the *Close Grammarly* button in the Ribbon.

Read Aloud and Immersive Reader

Word has a couple of nice features that you can use to help review your work to make sure your document is ready to be shared with the world, or at least your friend or coworkers.

The *Read Aloud* tool is used to read your document to you so that way you might be able to catch any mistakes or hear if something doesn't sound right. This tool can be found on the Review tab and when you click on it, Word will immediately start reading your document aloud starting where your cursor is located.

You can also highlight just the text that you want read to you with your mouse and after the selected text has been read, the Read Aloud tool will stop the reading process.

When you open the Read Aloud tool, you will see that there is a play button as well as a back and forward button. The back and forward buttons can be used to repeat the last section or skip forward to the next section within your document.

If you click on the settings gear icon, you can adjust the reading speed as well as choose between a female or male voice.

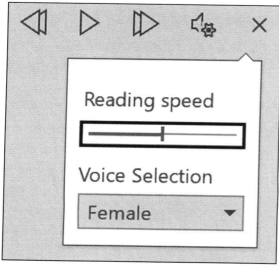

Figure 5.15

The *Immersive Reader* tool is used to help you focus specifically on what you are reading to avoid distractions. It can be found on the *View* tab and when you click on it, you will then get an *Immersive Reader* tab with several options. You will also notice that you can open the Read Aloud tool from here as well.

When you start the Immersive Reader, you will immediately notice that it will spread the words apart as well as make your paragraph width smaller.

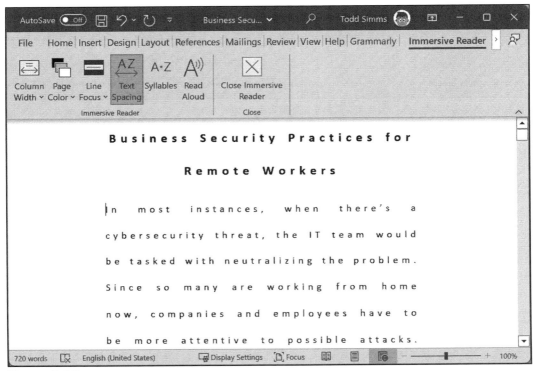

Figure 5.16

If you do not like the default setting, then there are several options that you can apply to your text to make the tool work better for you. You can change the column width, page color, line focus, text spacing and have the words broken down into syllables.

Figure 5.17 shows the syllables option turned on as well as the line focus set to three lines. As you can see, Word will display three lines at a time until you scroll your mouse or click the down arrow to show the next three lines. You can also set it to show one or five lines at a time.

The syllables in the words are separated by dots making it easier to sound out the words themselves.

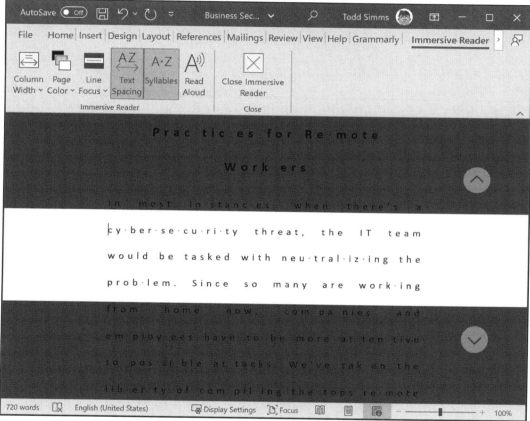

Figure 5.17

Word Count and Document Properties

Many times, when working on a document, you will have a requirement for it to be a minimum number of words or a maximum number of pages, etc. Fortunately, this is very easy to find in Word.

If you look at the bottom left corner of the Word interface, you will see a status bar that will list the number of pages as well as the number of words. This will update in real time as you add or remove content from your document.

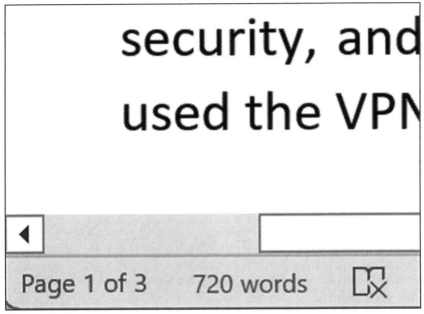

Figure 5.18

Another area to find this information as well as other information about your document is to go to the *File* tab and then the *Info* section (figure 5.19). Here you will find the same details about your document as well as many other attributes that you may or may not care about.

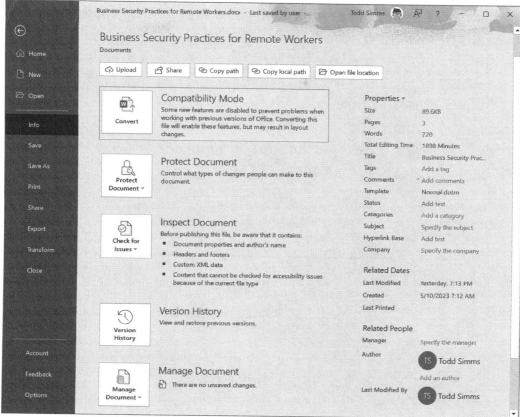

Figure 5.19

For example, if you were curious as to how much time you have spent working on your document, you can get that information in the *Total Editing Time* section. You can also see when your document was created, last modified and last printed.

The author name should have your name or the name of the person who the Word software belongs to if the document was created on your computer. You can change this if needed or add additional authors which might come in handy if you are sending your document out to other people and want them to know who worked on it.

Adding a Table of Contents

You might remember when I discussed the Navigation Pane how I mentioned that you can create a table of contents for your document by changing the outline level in the paragraph settings based on the structure of your document. This might be something you will never use but just in case you might, I will show you how to create a basic table of contents.

If I were to highlight the text for the chapter title, right click on it and choose *Paragraph*, I can then set the outline level to 1 since it's a top-level part of my table of contents.

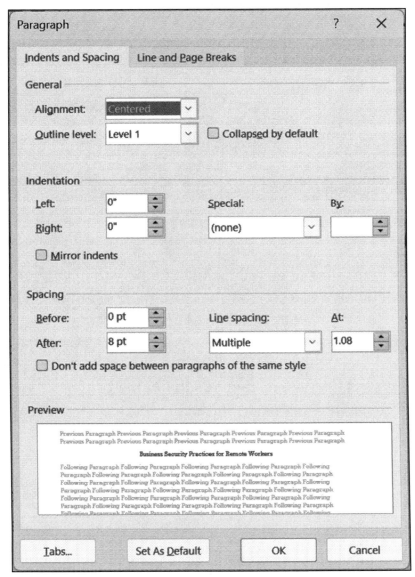

Figure 5.20

I can then do the same for any other top-level heading. Then for subtitles or subcategories, I can do the same process, but this time choose level 2. Then if I have some subcategories for the level 2 headings, I can make them level 3 and so on.

Before you create your table of contents, you will need to place the cursor where you want the TOC to be shown. Most likely this will be at the beginning of your document.

Next, you will need to go to the *References* tab and click on *Table of Contents*. Figure 5.21 shows that there are some built in formats from which you can choose. If you do not like any of these choices, you can click on *Custom Table of Contents* to configure your own.

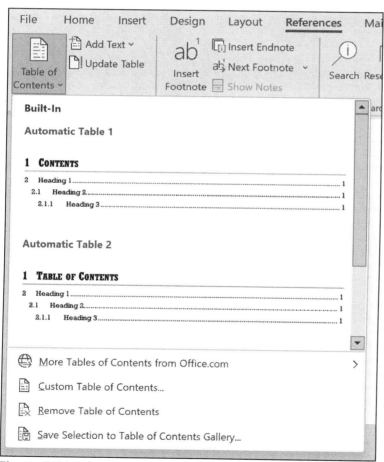

Figure 5.21

When you create a custom table of contents, you can choose whether or not to show page numbers, how many levels you want shown, and will also have the option to use hyperlinks instead of page numbers. This comes in handy when your readers will be viewing your document on a computer or other device because they can then click on the chapter or section and be taken directly to the page it starts on.

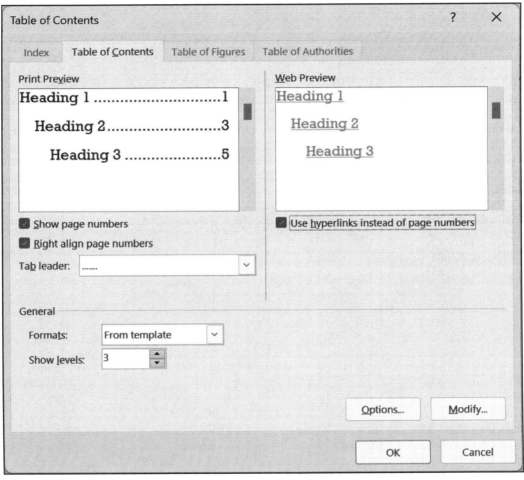

Figure 5.22

I have added level 1, 2 and 3 outline levels to my document and then created a custom TOC using the settings shown in figure 5.22. You can see the results in figure 5.23. You can see how each level is indented from the higher levels and how the level 3 lines are not bold compared to the level 1 and 2 lines.

Figure 5.23

Now if I were to open the Navigation Pane and go to the Headings section, I would be able to see each line that I had assigned an outline level to, and it will also indent each one based on its level number. I can then click on any of the headings to be taken to that section within my document.

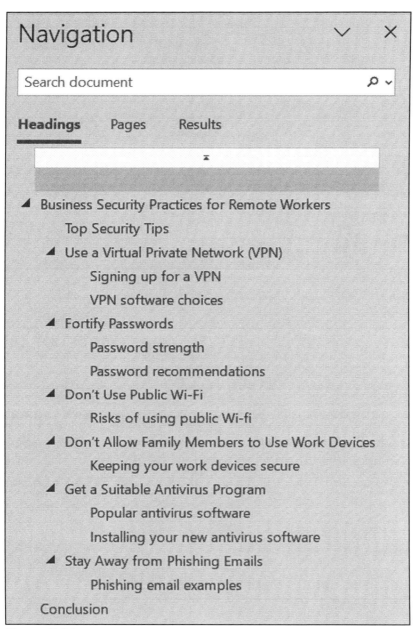

Figure 5.24

Chapter 6 – Printing, Sharing and Exporting

Once you have your document finalized and looking like it was written by a professional writer, you might have the need to do things such as print it out, email it, or share it with other people. No matter which way you prefer to get your document into the hands of others, it's going to be a fairly easy process to accomplish.

Printing

If you own a printer, then you have most likely printed out documents or photos from your computer and printing from Word is no different, at least when it comes to the initial printing process.

You may or may not have a print icon on your Quick Access bar depending on if you have added it or not. There are two types of print icons you can add here, and they are the *Quick Print* and the *Print Preview & Print* options.

Figure 6.1

The Quick Print option will simply start the printing process using the settings that were used to print the document last. So, if you had previously printed to your color printer and printed only the first three pages and made two copies of each, that is what you would get when you clicked on this button. If this is the first time you clicked on the

Quick Print button, then Word would print one copy of the entire document on your default printer.

The Print Preview & Print button will take you to the same print interface screen that you would see if you went to the *File* tab and then clicked on *Print* (figure 6.2). FYI, you can also use the keyboard shortcut **Ctrl-P** to get to this screen.

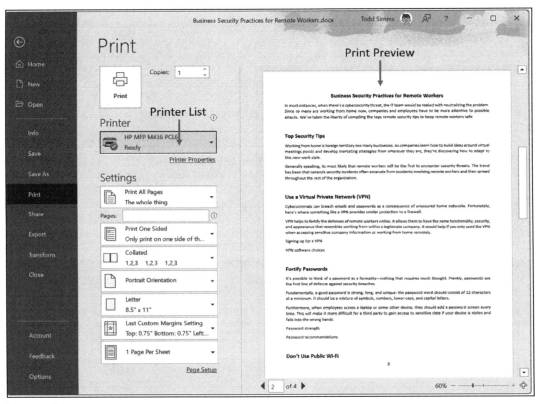

Figure 6.2

Even though it looks like there are a lot of options on this screen, there are only a few that you will most likely be using on a regular basis.

At the top, you will have the number of copies that you want to print and the default will be set to 1. The *Pages* box in the *Settings* section is important because that is where you will tell Word what pages you want to be printed if you do not want the entire document to be printed.

There are several ways to tell Word what pages you want to be printed. For example, if you wanted to print only pages 4 through 7 you would type **4-7** in the Pages box. If you wanted only pages 4,7 and 10 you would type **4,7,10** in the box. Another example would be if you wanted pages 4 through 7 and 10 you could type **4-7, 10**. If you wanted only odd pages or even pages to be printed, there is an option for that in the dropdown box above where it currently says *Print All Pages*.

The section at the top that says *Printer* will let you choose a different printer if you have more than one. Word should use your computer's default printer unless you tell it otherwise.

Over to the right of the screen you will have a preview of how your print job will look. You can use the page number arrows at the bottom of the preview to scroll through the pages to see them all if needed.

At the bottom of the Settings section, there is a link that you can click on that will take you to the page setup for that document. This is the same section you can get to from the Layout tab that I have already discussed.

Once you have everything configured correctly, simply click on the *Print* button at the top of the screen to start your print job.

Under the printer dropdown list, you will see a link that says *Printer Properties*. This can be used to adjust settings that are specific to your printer rather than to Word. The options you will have here will vary depending on your printer's make and model. Figure 6.3 shows the available settings for an HP LaserJet printer. You can see there are various tabs that can be used to change a variety of settings.

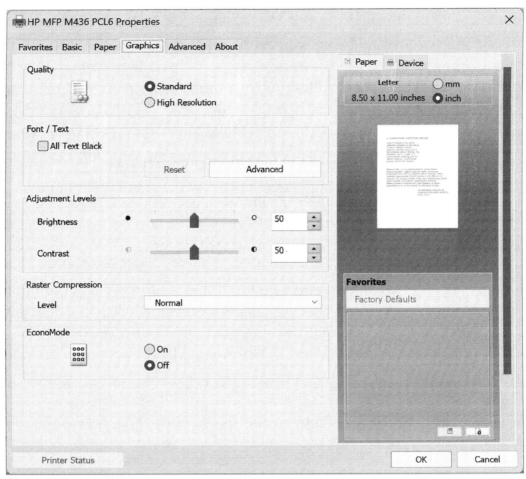

Figure 6.3

Sharing

There will most likely come a time when you will want to share your document with other people and printing it out and giving them a copy might not be possible. Plus, we all know that sending things electronically is a faster and more efficient process.

If you go to the *File* tab and then click on *Share*, you will have a limited number of sharing options that may or may not suit your needs. Your only real options are to upload it to your OneDrive online cloud storage account and share it from there or attach it to an email assuming you use Microsoft Outlook for your email client. If you use something else for your email such as Gmail, AOL, or Yahoo for example, you can attach your document to an email just like you would any other file attachment.

Figure 6.4

If your document is too large to email or if you want to share it with many people, you might want to try the OneDrive method. I will be going over OneDrive in more detail in chapter 7 but for now I will show you the steps on how to share your document using this process.

Before starting this process, you will need to make sure that you are logged into your OneDrive account which you most likely will be if you are using Windows. Microsoft tends to force OneDrive upon its users and sets up their account whether they want it or not! If you are not logged in, you should get prompted to do so.

There are two ways to share your document using OneDrive. You can have OneDrive send an email to one or more people inviting them to access your document or you can copy the sharing link that is provided to you and then paste it into your own email and send it to whomever you wish.

For my example, I will type in the email address of the person I want to share my document with. I will then add a message asking them to let me know what they think of my work.

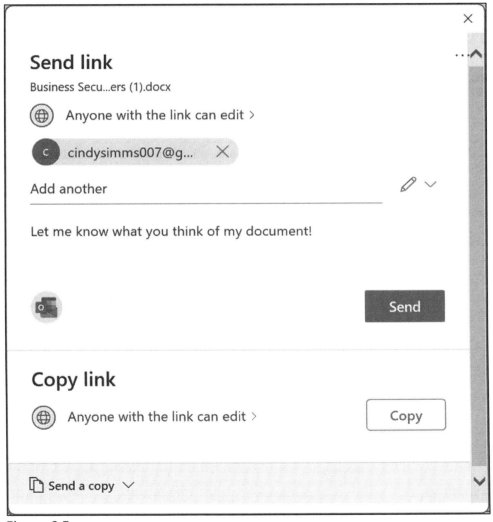

Figure 6.5

If you click on the pencil icon, you will be able to change the permission that the recipients have on your document from the default *editor* to *view only* if you do not want them to make any changes.

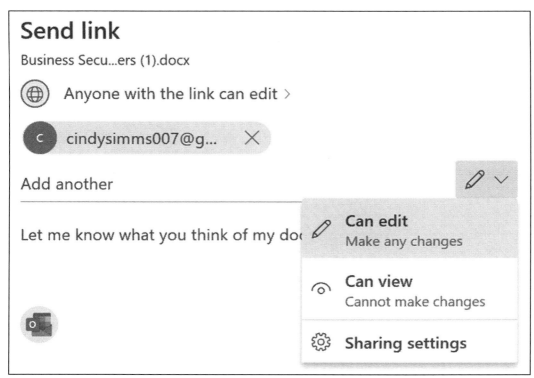

Figure 6.6

Once everything looks good, I will click the *Send* button to have the message sent to the people whose email addresses I have typed in.

Figure 6.7 shows how the document invitation email looks when opened by the recipient.

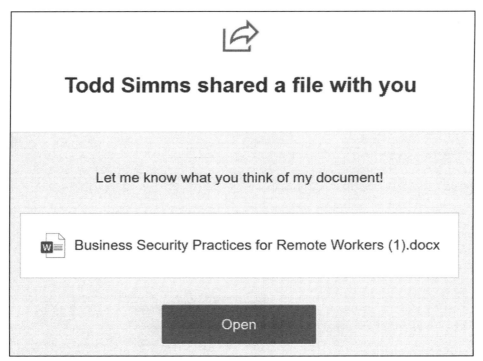

Figure 6.7

When they click on the *Open* button, the document will be opened from their OneDrive account in their web browser. They will then be able to work on it using the online version of Word or they can download it to their computer and then work on it using the desktop version of Word.

Creating a PDF Version of Your Document

PDF (Portable Document Format) files are a very popular or common type of file because they can be opened on almost any type of device including computers, smartphones and tablets. They are also popular because the file size is fairly small making them easy to email. Plus, you can make them so they cannot be edited without special software.

Word has two different ways to convert your document to a PDF file. One common way is to print your document to a PDF file. This process does not require you to have a physical printer because it's not really printing the document but rather converting it.

Microsoft includes a print to PDF virtual printer with their Windows operating system and you can use it with almost any program so it's not exclusive only to Word.

When you print your document, you can click on the printer selection dropdown and choose the *Microsoft Print to PDF* option and then click the *Print* button to start the process.

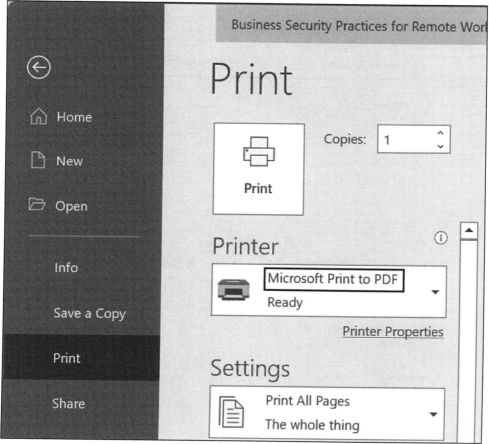

Figure 6.8

You will then be asked where on your computer you want to save your PDF file. You will also need to give your file a name. You can use the same name as your Word document if you choose to do so. Once you have the location selected and have typed in a name, simply click on the *Save* button to have your PDF file created.

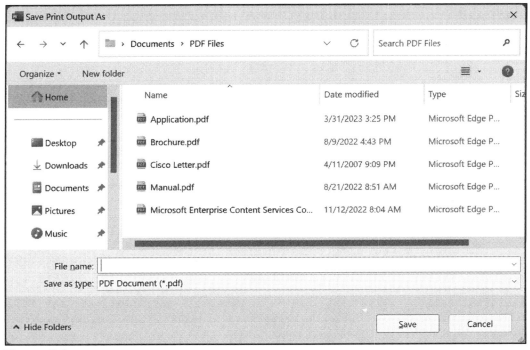

Figure 6.9

Another more advanced method to print a PDF involves exporting your document to a PDF file rather than printing it to one. To do this you will need to go to the *File* menu and choose the *Export* option.

Now you will need to make sure that the *Create PDF/XPS Document* option is selected and then you can click on the *Create PDF/XPS* button over to the right.

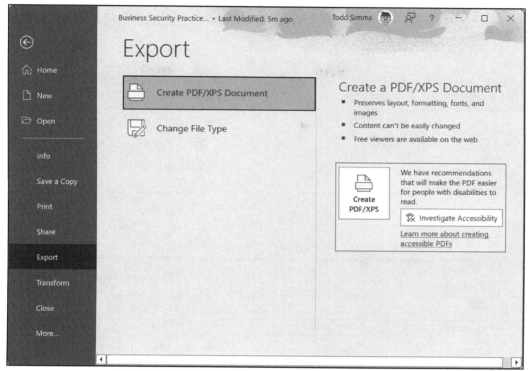

Figure 6.10

Once again, you will need to choose the location where you want to save your new PDF file. By default, Word will automatically give it the same name as the document you are printing with .pdf at the end rather than .docx. You can either keep this name or type in a new name for your new PDF file.

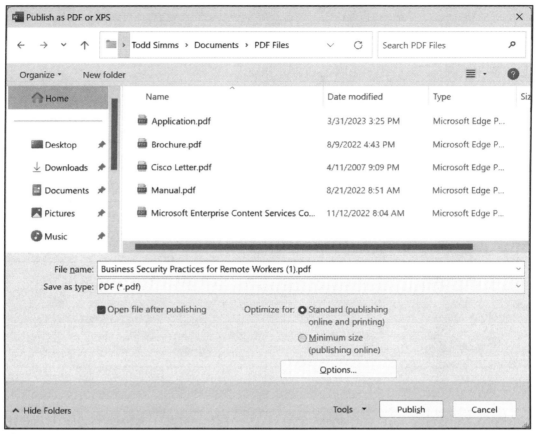

Figure 6.11

Depending on your needs, you can choose between *Standard* and *Minimum size* with Standard producing a higher quality PDF file at the cost of the PDF file being larger in size. Whichever option you choose, the PDF file shouldn't be too large unless you have a lot of images in your document.

If you click on the Options button (figure 6.12), you will have additional settings that you can configure for things such as printing only certain pages or options for custom printing at a publisher for example. Once you have your settings configured, you can click on the *Publish* button to have your PDF created.

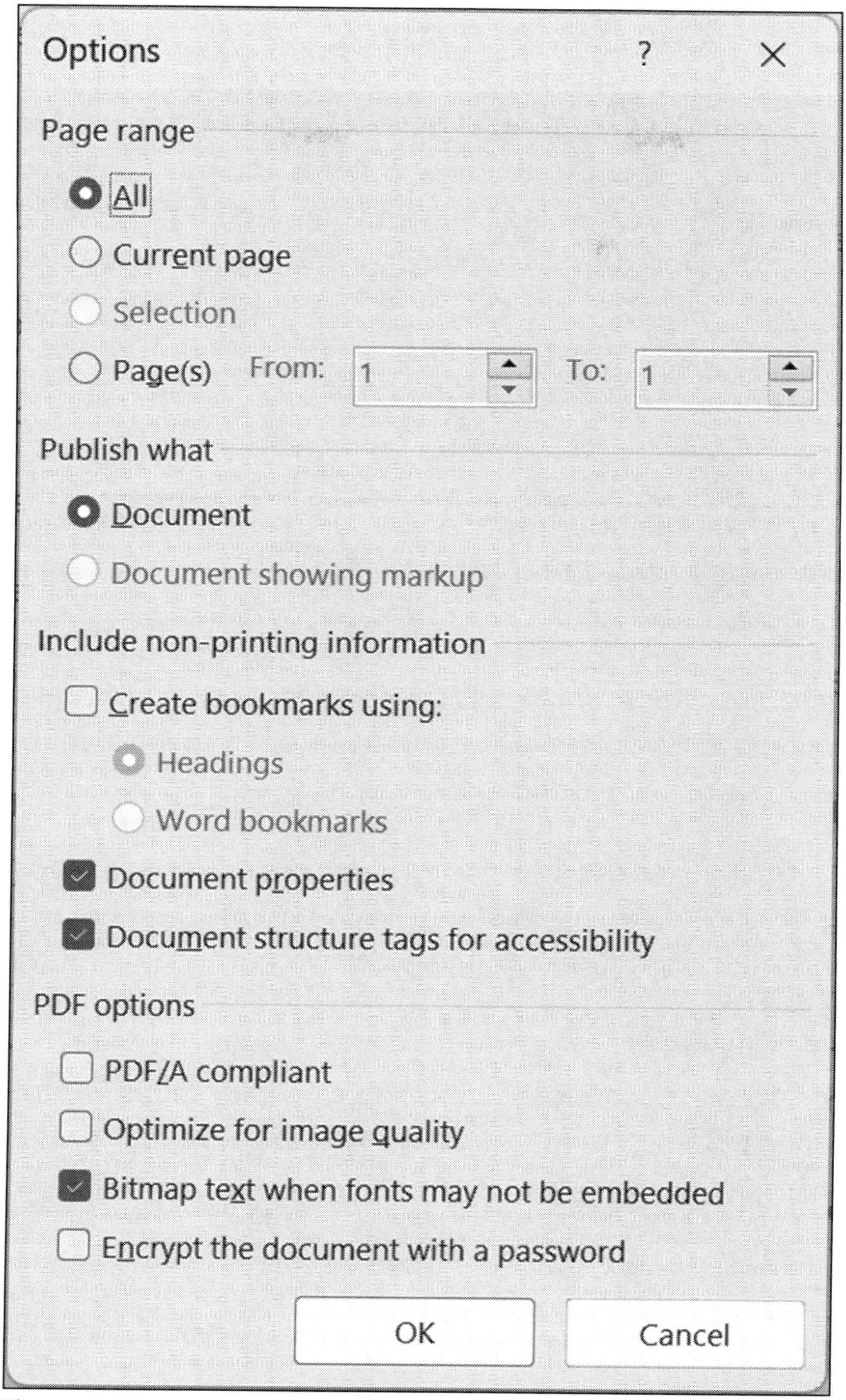

Options   ?   ✕

Page range

- ● All
- ○ Current page
- ○ Selection
- ○ Page(s) From: [1] ▲▼ To: [1] ▲▼

Publish what

- ● Document
- ○ Document showing markup

Include non-printing information

- ☐ Create bookmarks using:
  - ● Headings
  - ○ Word bookmarks
- ☑ Document properties
- ☑ Document structure tags for accessibility

PDF options

- ☐ PDF/A compliant
- ☐ Optimize for image quality
- ☑ Bitmap text when fonts may not be embedded
- ☐ Encrypt the document with a password

[OK]   [Cancel]

Figure 6.12

Chapter 7 – Extras

Now that you hopefully have a better understanding of how to use Word along with all its basic tools to create your documents, I wanted to take some time to go over some of the less common features that you didn't know you wanted to know about! Even if you don't think you will ever use the features discussed in this chapter, it might end up being helpful knowing they are available.

Tables

If you are familiar with Microsoft Excel which is used for making spreadsheets, then you might be wondering how you can apply that type of capability to your Word document.

Even though the main purpose of Excel is not to make tables, many people use it to do exactly that since it's a great tool to use to make lists to help you keep track of things such as inventory or even a chore list!

Word has the capability to insert tables into your document and you have several options when doing so. If you go to the *Insert* menu, you will see an icon called *Tables* and when you click on it, you will have several choices.

At the top, you can create a basic table by dragging your mouse to tell Word how many rows and columns you want to have added to this new table (figure 7.1).

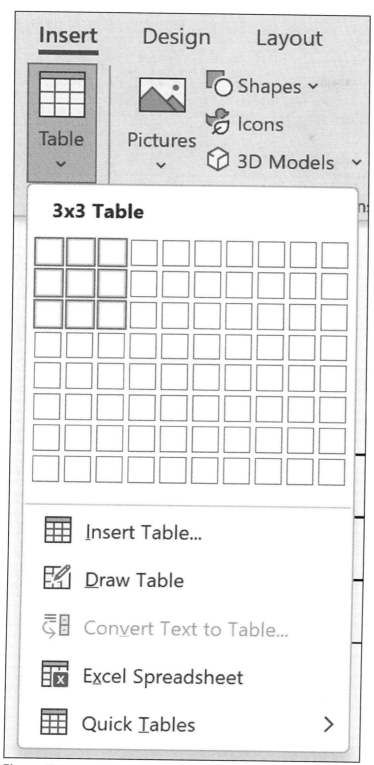

Figure 7.1

You can also click on *Insert Table* and type in the numbers manually.

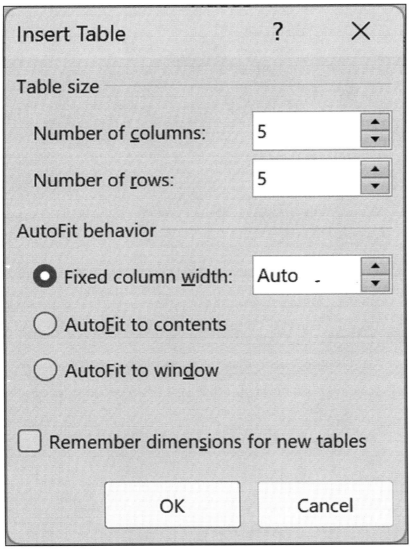

Figure 7.2

If you look at figure 7.3, you will see that you can even insert a basic Excel Spreadsheet into your document or choose a preconfigured table from the *Quick Tables* section.

Figure 7.3

For my example, I will insert a basic 3x3 table and figure 7.4 shows the results. You can click on any line within the table to shrink or expand the cells as needed if they are too big or too small. You will also notice that you have several tools in the *Table Design* bar that appears when you click on your new table. I will not be going over all of these tools, but you can play around with them to get an idea of what each one does.

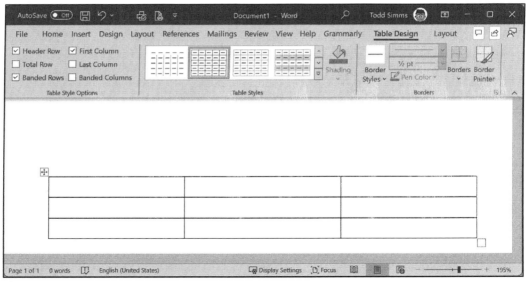

Figure 7.4

I have inserted some text into my table, and you can then format it like any other text in your document. You can also add fill colors to specific cells and change the border style. When you click on a cell to add or edit its contents, you should get a popup toolbar with formatting options as seen in figure 7.5.

Friday	Saturday	Sunday
Maria	Joe	Sandra
Dean	Phil	Jessie

Figure 7.5

You can also insert or remove rows or columns as needed with the *Insert* and *Delete* options.

Formatting Pictures

I had touched on the picture formatting options in chapter 2 but wanted to spend a little more time going over these options in more detail. When you insert a picture and then select it, you will then have a *Picture Format* tab with several groups contained within this tab.

You will also notice how you have circles on all four corners and the sides of your picture. These are where you would click and drag with your mouse to enlarge, shrink, stretch, or compress the picture. You can also use the curved arrow icon on the top to rotate the image.

Figure 7.6

The *Corrections* section has many preconfigured adjustments that you can choose from to do things such as sharpen, soften and change the brightness and contrast of your picture. You can click on any of them to have the setting instantly applied to your image.

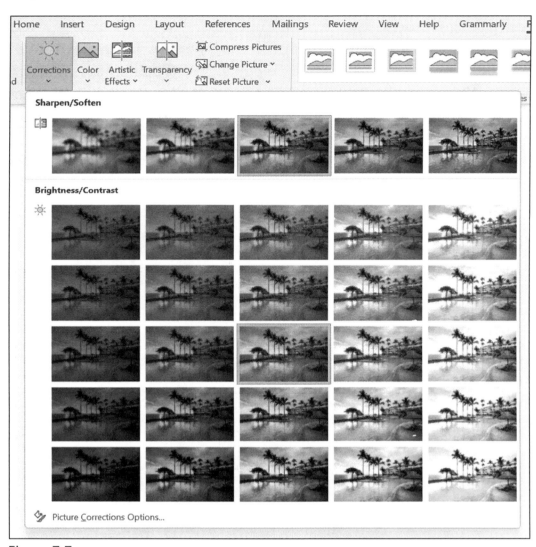

Figure 7.7

The *Color* section has many options to adjust color saturation and tone as well as some preconfigured custom color presets.

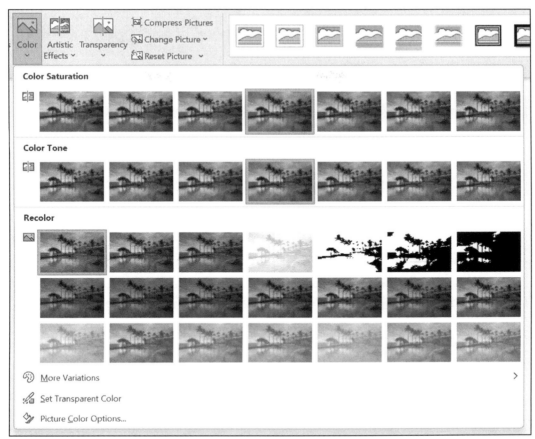

Figure 7.8

If you want to add a custom touch to your picture, you can try one of the settings from the *Artistic Effects* section.

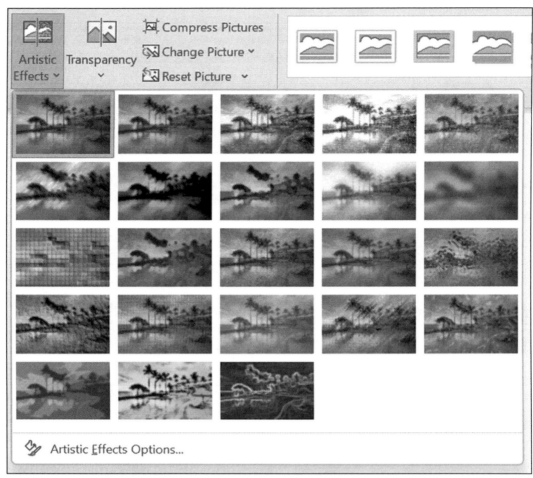

Figure 7.9

If you find that you have changed your picture too much and want to revert all the changes, simply click on the *Reset Picture* button.

If you would like to have a little more control over your picture adjustments, you can right click on the image and then choose *Format Picture*. Then over to the right of the screen you will have many options for adjustments such as borders, size, transparency, shadows, 3D effects, adding a text box, color, sharpness, cropping and so on (figure 7.10).

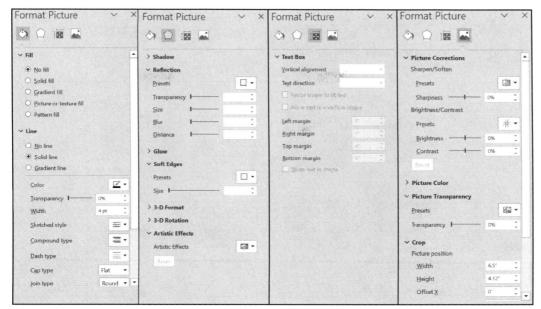

Figure 7.10

If you are looking for a way to add a little flair to your picture, you can click on *Picture Styles* to have one of the preconfigured settings applied to your picture (figure 7.11). Here you will find a variety of effects such as frames, shapes, shadows and 3D styles.

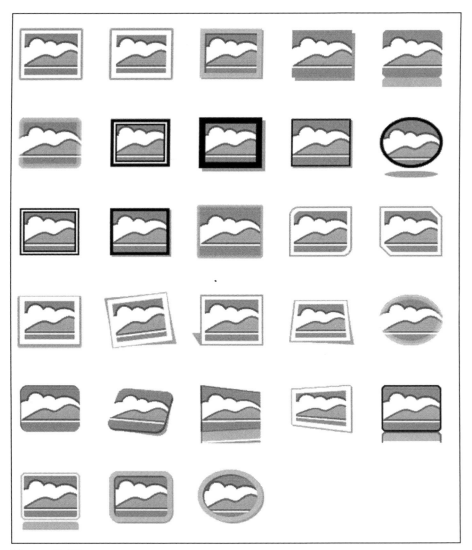

Figure 7.11

To see some additional styles broken down into categories, you can click on the *Picture Effects* section.

Figure 7.12

To add a simple or custom border to your picture you can click on the *Picture Border* option and configure your color and line choices before having them applied to your picture.

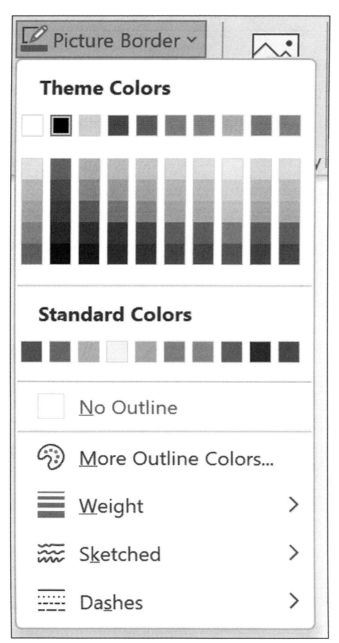

Figure 7.13

Figure 7.14 shows my picture with a custom border, glow effect and 3D rotation applied while figure 7.15 shows my picture when I used one of the default Picture Styles to make it look like a photograph.

Figure 7.14

Figure 7.15

Inserting Links

Most likely there have been several times when you have opened an email and it has contained a link that when clicked on takes you to a specific website on your computer. Or maybe it was even a picture that you can click on to take you to a website. Either way, these types of links can be inserted into your document to make it easy for your readers to access specific websites that you would like for them to check out.

Let's say you are creating a newsletter about your family vacation and want to include a link to the hotel you stayed at or maybe even a link to some photos that have been posted online. You can create these links within your text or picture with just a few simple steps.

To create a link, I suggest you first go to the website that you want to use for your link and copy the address from the address bar. Figure 7.16 shows a hotel website open in a web browser. To copy the address, you should be able to click within the address bar to have all the text highlighted. If it doesn't highlight everything, simply click in the box and press *Ctrl-A* on your keyboard to have all the text selected. If you miss any part of the address, then the link will not work when you use it in Word.

Figure 7.16

After you have the address text highlighted, right click on any area of the text, and choose the *Copy* option. This places the text on what is known as the clipboard which you can't see but will keep the last item you have copied handy and ready to paste wherever you need it.

Next, go to your Word document and highlight the text you want to turn into a link. If you want a picture to become a link, you can click on it to select it instead. Right click either the highlighted text or the picture and choose the *Link* option.

Figure 7.17

You will then be presented with the *Insert Hyperlink* dialog box and there are two main areas you need to be concerned with. The first one is the *Text to display* box. This will automatically be filled in with the text you highlighted and if you change it, then the text in your document will be changed as well. This option will be greyed out (inactive) if you are right clicking on a picture.

The box next to the word *Address* is where you will paste in the website address that you copied in the previous step. If you are wondering why you are also seeing files and folders in the middle of this box, that is because you can link to other files within your document but that is a more advanced topic.

Once you have your address pasted into the box, simply click on the *OK* button and the text or image you selected will now be a clickable link (figure 7.19).

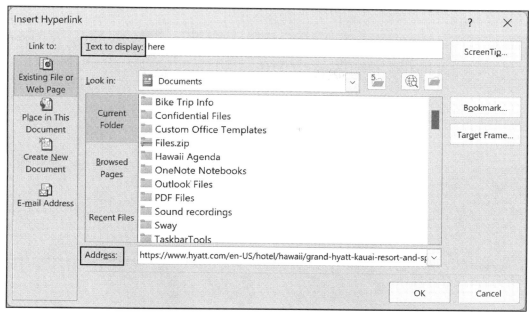

Figure 7.18

Now when someone is reading your document on their computer or other device, they can click on the text link to be taken to the website you specified in the previous step. If you are printing out your document, the text will just show up as blue and underlined but obviously you can't click on a link from a piece of paper!

Here is a picture of the hotel we stayed at in Hawaii. It was a great place to stay and actually not too expensive! If you want to check it out for your upcoming trip you can click here to go to the website.

Figure 7.19

OneDrive

When saving and even opening documents, you might have noticed that Word will ask you if you want to save to your OneDrive online account. OneDrive is an online cloud storage service that all Windows users get for free and many times Microsoft will automatically configure your account the first time you log into your computer.

Figure 7.20

When you use OneDrive to store your files, that makes them accessible from any device such as a computer, smartphone, or tablet that has an internet connection. Therefore, you can access your files while on vacation, at work, on the road and so on. It can also act as a backup for your files if you want to have a copy online as well as on your computer's hard drive.

One downside to this is that you might be saving some files online in OneDrive and other times saving them to your computer and not realizing which location has which files. With that said, you will need to pay attention to where you are saving your files but should only need to worry about it the first time you save one because each time you click the Save button after that, Word will save your file to the same location.

If you would like to check out your online OneDrive account to see if you have anything in there or even start using it, then you can go to the website at https://onedrive.live.com/. You will need to log in with your Microsoft account which is most likely the same email address and password you use on your computer. If you do not know this information you can use the *forgot password* option to get yourself logged in.

Once you are logged in, you will see a section called *My files* that may or may not have any files or folders within it. Over at the left you will have additional sections for recently accessed files, photos, files shared with others and deleted files.

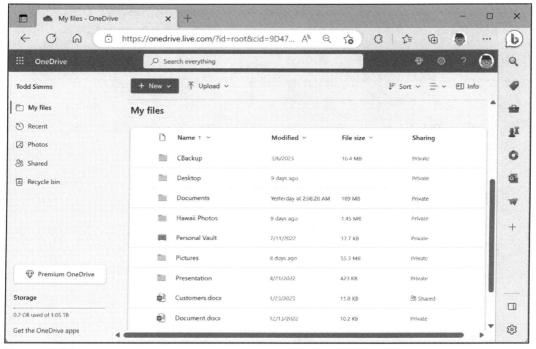

Figure 7.21

At the top, you will find a button that says *New* if you want to create a new folder or online Word document etc. The *Upload* button is used to upload files or folders from your computer to your online storage location. It will not move them there but rather just make a copy of them in your OneDrive account.

Once you have files uploaded to your account, you can then view and even edit many of them online. One benefit of having your files online is that you can easily share them with one or more people without having to email them a copy.

There is a lot you can do with OneDrive, but I just wanted to give you a basic overview in case you wanted to check it out in more detail later.

Word Ruler

When creating documents that contain objects such as pictures, tables, or other graphics, you might find that you need to know what size these objects are on the page itself. Let's say you have two pictures, and you want to make sure that they are exactly the same size without having to go by only what you see on the screen.

Word has a built-in ruler that you can use for this purpose but there is a good chance that it might not be enabled. Figure 7.22 shows a document with an image, and I want to make sure that the picture is no larger than 4 inches wide in size.

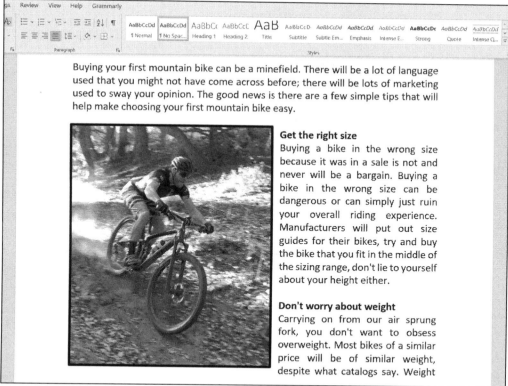

Figure 7.22

To enable the ruler, you can go to the *View* tab and check the *Ruler* checkbox in the *Show* group (figure 7.23). As you can see, my picture is about 3.5 inches wide so I am less than my 4-inch limit.

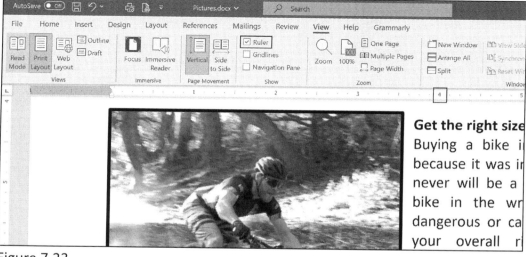

Figure 7.23

Word will set the ruler to start at the upper left margin for each page as seen in figure 7.24 rather than the edge of the actual page so be aware of that when making your measurements. The grey section of the ruler represents the page margin.

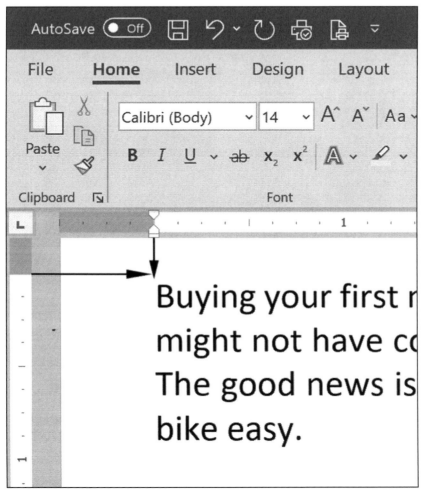

Figure 7.24

If you want to change the unit of measurement for the ruler to something else besides inches, you can go to the Word options by clicking on the *File* tab, *Options*, *Advanced* and then find the *Display* section. Then where it says *Show measurements in units of*, you can change it to centimeters, millimeters, points, or picas.

Word Options

General	**Display**		
Display			
Proofing	Show this number of Recent Documents:	50	ⓘ
Save	☐ Quickly access this number of Recent Documents:	4	
Language	Show this number of unpinned Recent Folders:	50	
Accessibility	Show measurements in units of:	Inches ⌄	
Advanced	Style area pane width in Draft and Outline views:	Inches	
Customize Ribbon	☐ Show pixels for HTML features	Centimeters	
Quick Access Toolbar	☑ Show shortcut keys in ScreenTips	Millimeters	
	☑ Show horizontal scroll bar	Points	
Add-ins	☑ Show vertical scroll bar	Picas	
Trust Center	☑ Show vertical ruler in Print Layout view		
	☐ Optimize character positioning for layout rather than readability		
	☑ Update document content while dragging ⓘ		
	☑ Use subpixel positioning to smooth fonts on screen		
	☑ Show pop-up buttons for adding rows and columns in tables		

Figure 7.25

Thesaurus

Word comes with a built-in thesaurus to help you find synonyms, or similar words, for a particular word. To get to the thesaurus, simply go to the *Review* tab and you will find it in the *Proofing* group.

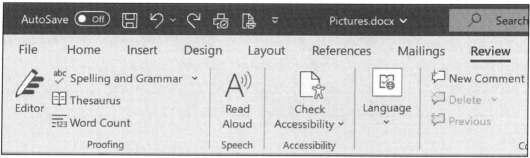

Figure 7.26

If you highlight the word you want to look up in the thesaurus before clicking on the thesaurus button, it will automatically be added into the search box and show you instant results.

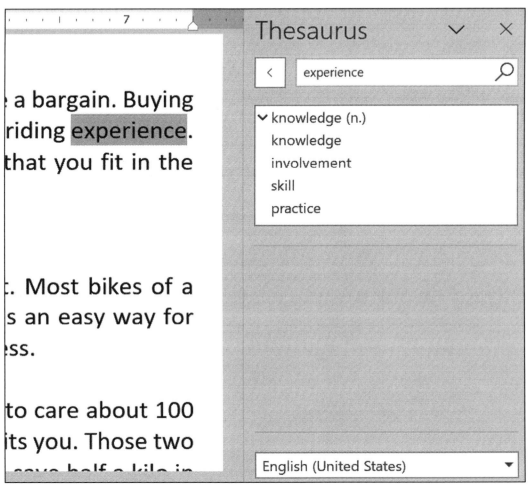

Figure 7.27

You can also right click on a highlighted word and choose *Synonyms* and if you want to replace your word with one of the suggestions, you can simply click on it. You can also click on *Thesaurus* from here to open the same Thesaurus interface as seen before.

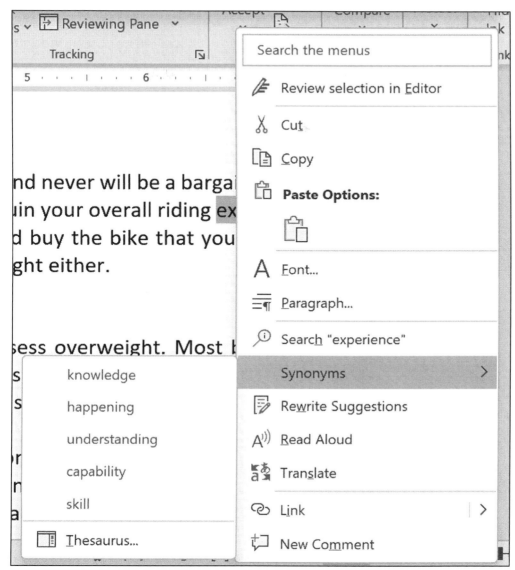

Figure 7.28

Searching\Find and Replace

You may recall that you are able to search within your document from the Navigation Pane that I discussed in chapter 5. But if you need to do a more advanced search or even replace one word with another throughout your entire document, you can do so from the *Editing* tools found within the *Home* tab.

There are three options to choose from within the Editing tools and they are *Find, Replace* and *Select*. For now, I will be focusing on the Find and Replace options.

Figure 7.29

If you click on the dropdown arrow next to Find, you will have the basic Find option which will open the Navigation Pane. The *Advanced Find* option will open the *Find and Replace* feature which is the same as clicking on the Replace button from figure 7.29. The *Go To* option will also open the Find and Replace box with the Go To tab active.

Figure 7.30

Once you have the Find and Replace tool open, you will see that you can do a basic search for words or phrases and even filter your searches on things such as capitalization and whole words. If you have a specific word highlighted within your document when you open the search feature, that word will automatically be added to the search box. You can then click on the *Find Next* button to show you each instance of that word within your document.

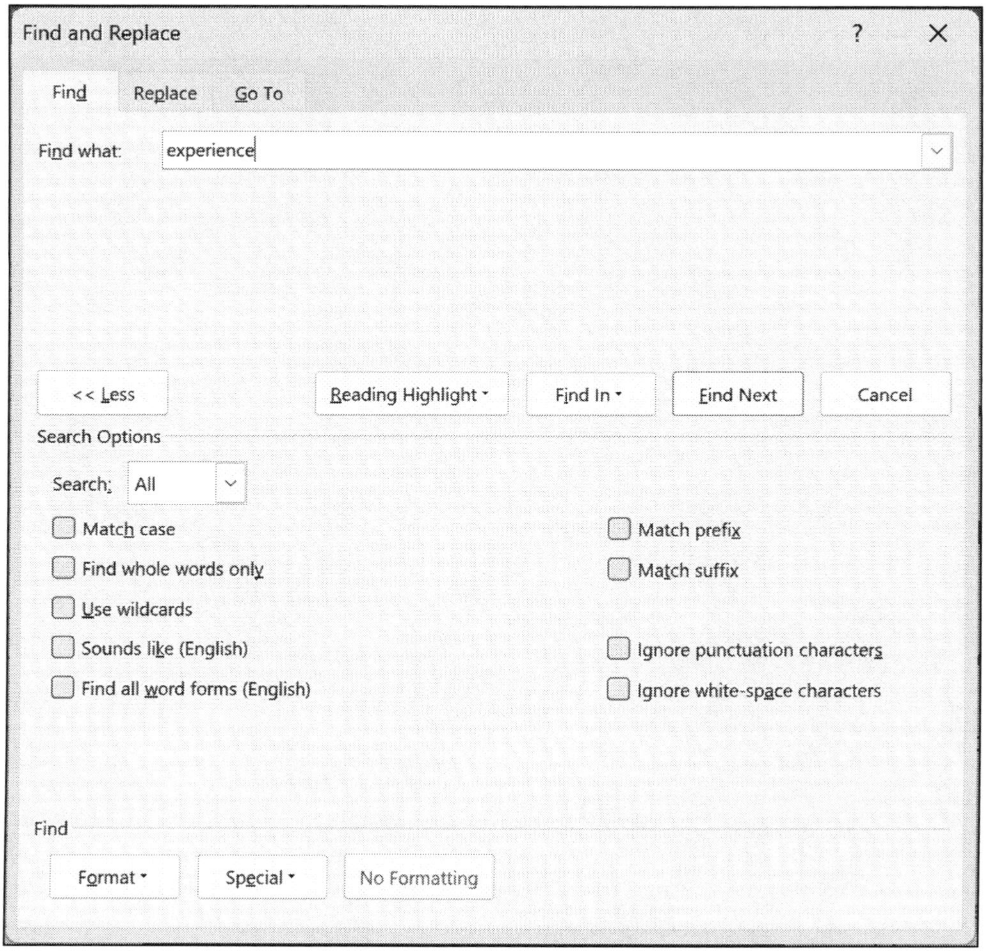

Figure 7.31

If you would like to replace a word with a different word, you can click on the *Replace* tab and type in the word you want to search for and then the word you want to replace it with. You can replace the first instance it finds and keep replacing the specific word one at a time or you can click on the *Replace All* button to have all the instances of that word replaced.

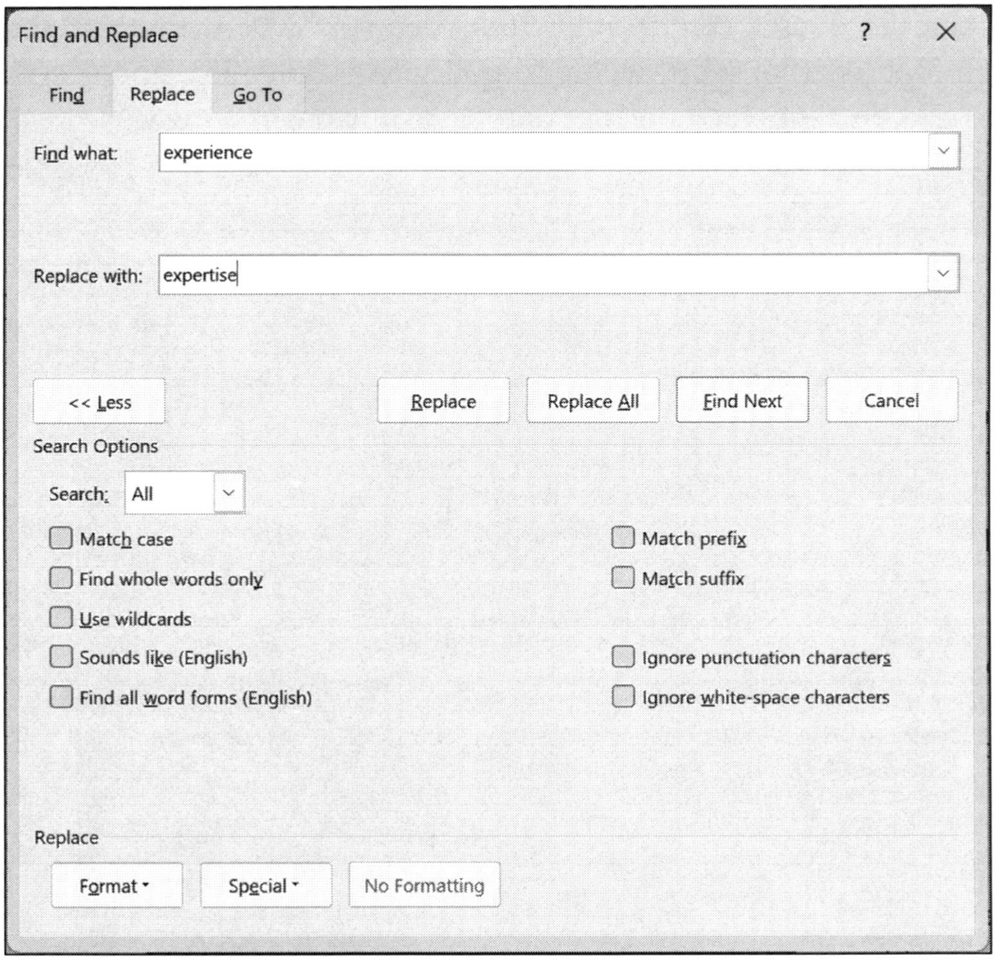

Figure 7.32

The *Go To* section is used to take you to a specific place within your document. This comes in handy if you have a large document and would rather not scroll to say page 250 but rather just type it in the box and click on the *Next* button.

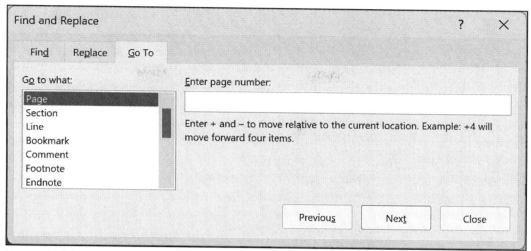

Figure 7.33

Options

Like most software, Word has a variety of options that you can configure to change how the program works. There is a good chance you will never need to change any of these options, but I wanted to take a moment to show you how to get to them and show you what kinds of adjustments you can make from here.

To get to the Word options, click on the *File* tab and then on *Options*. You will then see all the available categories for the settings that you can change within the software.

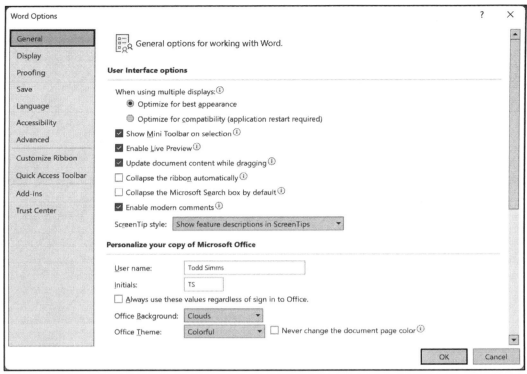

Figure 7.34

Here is a very brief overview of what settings you will find in these categories.

- **General** – Used to personalize your copy of Word and change some settings for the user interface.

- **Display** – Tells Word how to show pages on the screen, whether or not to show formatting markers and other data on the screen and when printing.

- **Proofing** – Here you can adjust how your document is checked for errors regarding grammar and spelling. You can also adjust autocorrect settings.

- **Save** – If you want to change how Word saves your document such as the default save location as well as do things such as turn on the Autosave feature, you can do so from here.

- **Language** – By default, Word will use the language that is configured on your computer but also allows you to add additional languages if needed.

- **Accessibility** – This section contains settings that are used to make your document easier to read for people with disabilities.

- **Advanced** – Here you will find the bulk of the Word settings that apply to things like editing, copying, links, images, printing and so on.

- **Customize Ribbon** – If you want to customize how the Ribbon works by adding or removing features, you can do so from here.

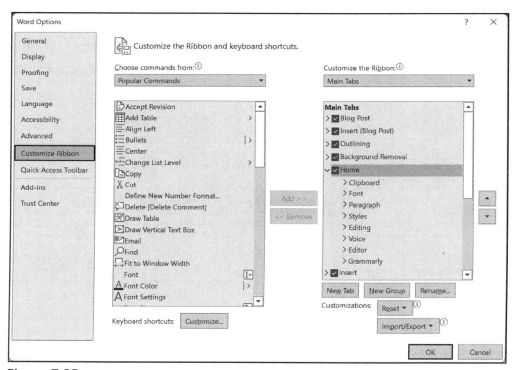

Figure 7.35

- **Quick Access Toolbar** – You can customize the Quick Access Toolbar the same way as you can for the Ribbon in this section.

- **Add-ins** – Word will come with its own add-ins in addition to any that you might install yourself. If an add-in is affecting how Word is running, you can come here to disable it to see if that helps the problem.

- **Trust Center** – In this section, you can adjust various security settings for trusted publishers, add-ins, macros and so on.

Help

While using Word, you will most likely run into a situation where you need to figure out how to perform a certain task or maybe want a little training on how to use a particular feature etc.

Word has a *Help* tab that you can access to find answers to your questions, chat with Microsoft support and find training on a variety of subjects.

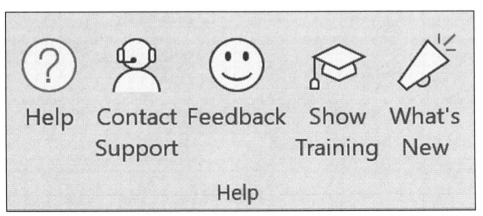

Figure 7.36

When you click on the *Help* icon, you will be shown several suggested topics that you can then browse to find the answer to your question.

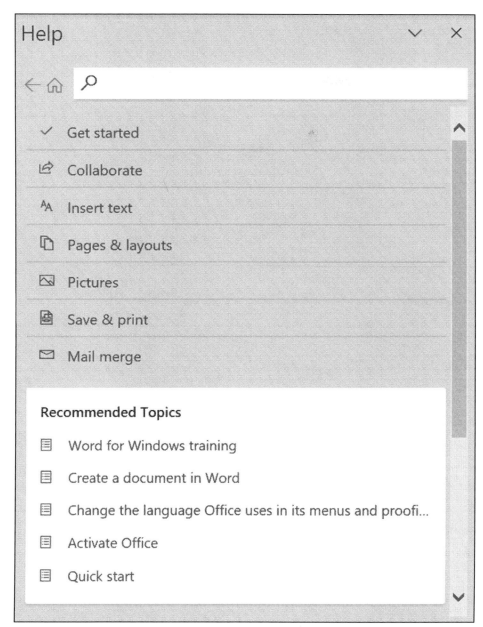

Figure 7.37

If none of them suit your needs, you can then type in a specific word or question in the search box and then go through the results that are shown after you press enter on your keyboard.

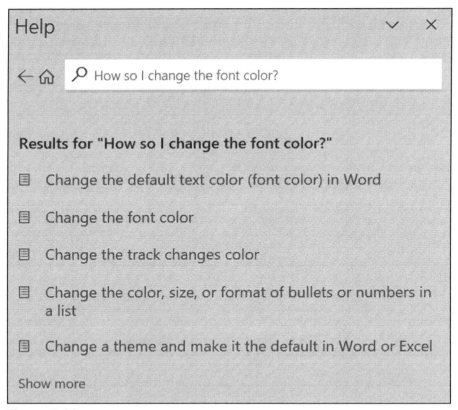

Figure 7.38

The *Contact Support* option will let you start a chat with Microsoft support to see if they can help you with your issue or question. You will need to sign into your Microsoft account to use this feature so make sure you know the email address and password associated with your account.

If you are looking for some additional training on a specific topic, you can click on the *Training* button to be shown a variety of topics that you can then choose from (figure 7.39). The format of the training will be reading material and video based.

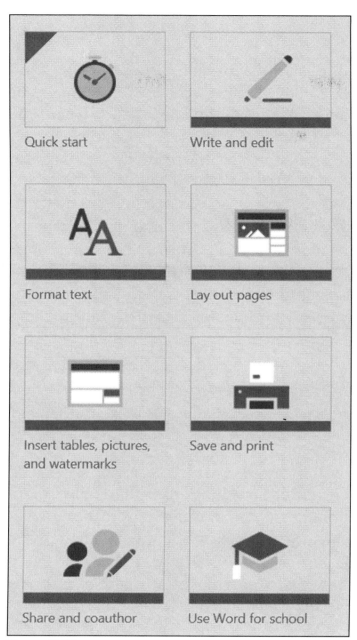

Figure 7.39

What's Next?

Now that you have read through this book and learned how Microsoft Word works and what you can do with the application, you might be wondering what you should do next. Well, that depends on where you want to go. Are you happy with what you have learned, or do you want to further your knowledge of the available Microsoft Office apps such as Excel and PowerPoint and become an Office expert?

If you do want to expand your knowledge and computers in general, then you can look for some more advanced books on basic computers or focus on a specific technology such as Windows, Google Apps, or DropBox, if that is the path you choose to follow. Focus on mastering the basics, and then apply what you have learned when going to more advanced material.

There are many great video resources as well, such as Pluralsight or CBT Nuggets, which offer online subscriptions to training videos of every type imaginable. YouTube is also a great source for instructional videos if you know what to search for.

If you are content in being a proficient Word user that knows more than your coworkers and friends, then just keep on practicing what you have learned. Don't be afraid to poke around with some of the settings and tools that you normally don't use and see if you can figure out what they do without having to research it since learning by doing is the most effective method to gain new skills.

Thanks for reading **Microsoft Word for Seniors Made Easy**. You can also check out the other books in the Made Easy series for additional computer related information and training. You can get more information on my other books on my Computers Made Easy Book Series website.

https://www.madeeasybookseries.com/

You should also check out my computer tips website, as well as follow it on Facebook to find more information on all kinds of computer topics.

www.onlinecomputertips.com
https://www.facebook.com/OnlineComputerTips/

About the Author

James Bernstein has been working with various companies in the IT field for over 20 years, managing technologies such as SAN and NAS storage, VMware, backups, Windows Servers, Active Directory, DNS, DHCP, Networking, Microsoft Office, Photoshop, Premiere, Exchange, and more.

He has obtained certifications from Microsoft, VMware, CompTIA, ShoreTel, and SNIA, and continues to strive to learn new technologies to further his knowledge on a variety of subjects.

He is also the founder of the website onlinecomputertips.com, which offers its readers valuable information on topics such as Windows, networking, hardware, software, and troubleshooting. James writes much of the content himself and adds new content on a regular basis. The site was started in 2005 and is still going strong today.

Made in the USA
Columbia, SC
18 December 2024

49808905R00111